LIZ CURTIS HIGGS

Slightly Bad Girls of the Bible

Flawed Women Loved by a Flawless God

WATERBROOK
PRESS

SLIGHTLY BAD GIRLS OF THE BIBLE WORKBOOK
PUBLISHED BY WATERBROOK PRESS
12265 Oracle Boulevard, Suite 200
Colorado Springs, Colorado 80921

All Scripture quotations, unless otherwise indicated, are taken from the Holy Bible, New International Version®. NIV®. Copyright © 1973, 1978, 1984 by International Bible Society. Used by permission of Zondervan Publishing House. All rights reserved. Scripture quotations marked (ICB) are taken from the International Children's Bible®. Copyright © 1986, 1988, 1999 by Thomas Nelson Inc. Used by permission. All rights reserved. Scripture quotations marked (KJV) are taken from the King James Version. Scripture quotations also taken from The Message by Eugene H. Peterson. Copyright © 1993, 1994, 1995, 1996, 2000, 2001, 2002. Used by permission of NavPress Publishing Group. All rights reserved. Scripture quotations marked (NLT) are taken from the Holy Bible, New Living Translation, copyright © 1996. Used by permission of Tyndale House Publishers Inc., Wheaton, Illinois 60189. All rights reserved.

ISBN 978-1-4000-7213-2

Published in the United States by WaterBrook Multnomah, an imprint of the Crown Publishing Group, a division of Random House Inc., New York.

WATERBROOK and its deer colophon are registered trademarks of Random House Inc.

Printed in the United States of America
2014

10 9

Contents

Introduction: *Good Girls Behaving Badly* 1

One: *A Matter of Time* 3
Sarai

Two: *Flight Plan* 21
Hagar

Three: *The Last Laugh* 37
Sarah

Four: *A Willful Bride* 55
Rebekah the Wife

Five: *Using Her Wits* 73
Rebekah the Mother

Six: *The Night Has Eyes* 89
Leah the Unseen

Seven: *Morning Has Broken* 107
Leah the Unloved

Eight: *When All Is Said and Done* 121
Rachel

A Last Word from Liz 139

Good Girls Behaving Badly

S is, you've already earned a Good Girl badge for your willingness to dig deeper into God's Word. Bless you for joining me!

Whether you identify with Sarah's impatience, Hagar's mean-girl streak, Rebekah's take-charge personality, Leah's longing for love, or Rachel's envy of another woman's blessings, I promise you'll connect at a deeply personal level with one or more of these Slightly Bad Girls. And should you discover bits of yourself in *all* of them, as I have, don't fret. God loved these five women, even as he loves us—not in spite of our flaws, but because of them. For proof, check out Romans 5:8! *God demonstrates his own love for us in this: while we were still sinners, Christ died for us.*

If you're reading *Slightly Bad Girls of the Bible* on your own, the workbook lets us sit side by side as I guide you through each chapter of these women's lives. If you're using the book and workbook in a small-group setting, think of me as an unseen sister cheering you on and helping you delve further into the biblical material.

You'll find plenty of personal-application questions here as well. With prayer and a willing heart, ask the Lord to show you what he wants you to learn from your past experiences, including those (gulp) you'd rather not look at. Examine them honestly in light of the Scriptures, then rejoice as the Lord washes you clean of any lingering shame. As the apostle Paul told the churches in Galatia, "What counts is a new creation" (Galatians 6:15).

The questions posed at the end of each chapter of *Slightly Bad Girls of the Bible* are included (and greatly expanded) in the workbook. If your penmanship, like mine, is larger than average, take heart: Paul once wrote, "See what large letters I use as I write to you with my own hand!" (Galatians 6:11). I've allowed lots of room to jot down responses, comments, insights, doodles—whatever helps you process and absorb the truths we'll be exploring together.

I'd recommend reading one chapter of the *Slightly Bad Girls* book at a time, then answering the corresponding workbook questions. You may find you'll gain more by completing one or two questions a day rather than hurriedly jotting down all your answers an hour before your Bible-study group meets. (I have *so* been there.) The goal here is personal growth, not pages full of ink, so take your time and savor the journey.

In addition to this companion workbook, you'll need (1) your own copy of the book *Slightly Bad Girls of the Bible*, (2) your favorite Bible (any translation is fine—you'll find the New International Version primarily quoted here), and (3) your favorite pen or pencil. Please don't obsess over finding the "right" answer, beloved. The Lord alone knows what you need to learn; you can trust his leading.

Get ready for a novel approach to Bible study as we explore the lives of five ancient females who are here to teach us how God works through strong-willed women!

Thank you for the investment of time, energy, thought, study, and personal vulnerability to touch our hearts and change our lives. It was a privilege to facilitate your Bible study and see the impact.

Darla from Florida

A Matter of Time

Sarai

Four thousand years ago Sarai's biological clock was ticking louder by the hour. Our midlife matriarch feared she might *never* give birth. So Sarai did what Slightly Bad Girls do: she took the matter into her own hands instead of trusting God to honor his word. Sarai soon learned a hard lesson (is there any other kind?), demonstrating for her twenty-first-century sisters the value of waiting on the Lord.

1a. Before we open God's Word, let's take a look at our preconceived notions of Sarai/Sarah, if only so we might sweep them away and meet the real woman. What was your opinion of Sarai *before* you studied her story in Genesis 11–16? On what was that image based? *Disbelief in the Lord for she would bear a child*

b. And what do you think of Sarai now? What surprises you most about her?

c. When we first meet Sarai in **Genesis 11:29–30**, we learn she is barren. How would that have made life difficult for Sarai as a woman and particularly as Abram's wife?

d. Our perspectives and behaviors are greatly affected by places and events in our lives. Note how each of the following aspects of Sarai's life might have shaped her Slightly Bad Girl self.

Her years in prosperous Ur:

Her nomadic life with Abram:

Her experience in Pharaoh's harem:

e. Now it's your turn. List three significant places and/or events in your life and how they contributed to the woman you are today.

Seeing these benchmarks in print, what fresh insights do you gain about yourself?

f. Sarai's marriage to Abram surely had the greatest impact on her life. Based on your personal experience or observation, what are the blessings of being married to a man uniquely called by God? And what are the challenges?

g. In **1 Timothy 3:1–9** we find a laundry list of God's expectations for a man in spiritual leadership. Jot down one requirement from each verse. If there are several, choose the one you think might be the hardest to manage.

1 Timothy 3:2 – self-controlled

1 Timothy 3:3 – not a lover of money

1 Timothy 3:4-5 – children obey him w/ proper respect.

1 Timothy 3:6 – he must not be a recent convert

1 Timothy 3:7

1 Timothy 3:8

1 Timothy 3:9

How does Abram measure up to this list?

What impact would those qualities have had on Sarai's life?

h. Wives of godly men face expectations too. According to the following verses, in what ways should a virtuous wife honor her husband?

Proverbs 31:11–12

Colossians 3:18

1 Timothy 3:11

How does Sarai compare to the preceding description?

And how do you compare?

> Sarai was part of God's plan for Abram from the beginning, though she didn't know it yet.
>
> Liz Curtis Higgs in *Slightly Bad Girls of the Bible*, page 17

2a. Sarai is the first woman in Scripture described as barren, though she would certainly not be the last. Since "children are a gift from the LORD" (**Psalm 127:3**, NLT), to what end might God have closed Sarai's womb for a long season?

b. What hope do **Psalm 103:13, Isaiah 49:13,** and **James 5:11** offer as we persevere through our own seasons of disappointment?

c. What assurance does **Luke 1:36–37** provide, not only for women who wish to give birth, but for any of us who have unmet longings?

d. In **Isaiah 54:1–5** God's people are compared to a barren woman. Whether we're praying for a husband, for a child, or for a fresh start, what does this passage reveal about the hope the Lord offers those who desire his blessing?

And how might these verses—the last one especially—encourage you?

Isaiah 54:4

Isaiah 54:5

e. Is marriage still a source of esteem for women? Is childbearing? Why or why not?

f. What are some ways modern society measures the worth of a woman?

g. How do you measure your own worth? And what comfort do you find in **Matthew 10:29–31**?

h. According to **Acts 20:24,** how did the apostle Paul measure his worth?

If you share Paul's passion, how does your life testify "to the gospel of God's grace"?

> It wasn't Sarai's inability to conceive that made her a
> Slightly Bad Girl. Not for one minute. In fact, her childless
> state made room for a miracle.
>
> **Liz Curtis Higgs in *Slightly Bad Girls of the Bible*, page 15**

3a. Abram and Sarai left everything—family and friends, houses and
lands, and all their worldly goods that wouldn't fit on a camel—to
follow God's leading. According to **Genesis 12:1,** what three things
did the Lord ask Abram to leave behind?

b. Where specifically was God sending him? What challenges might
such a destination have presented?

c. What assurance does **Isaiah 58:11** offer those who follow God
in new directions, as this brave couple did? What did Abram and
Sarai need beyond having their physical requirements met?

d. If the Lord asked you to leave everything and follow his lead, how
would you respond? What questions would you need answered?
And how eager would you be to go?

e. Isaiah's response to God's call on his life is captured in a single, powerful verse. Read **Isaiah 6:8.** What did the Lord ask? And how did the prophet respond?

f. Now let's step back a few verses. Before God could send Isaiah, something life changing had to happen. Read **Isaiah 6:1–7.** What problem was revealed to Isaiah? And how did God solve it?

unholiness, he sent an angel

g. We know Abram and Sarai were far from perfect. Just like Isaiah. And just like us. Think of a time when you cried, "Woe to me!" or some modern equivalent—"I've blown it" or "I'm worthless" or, as The Message phrases **Isaiah 6:5,** "I'm as good as dead!" How does God's solution for Isaiah's "unclean lips" assure you that God can handle your sin and guilt?

h. God's calling has not changed since Abram and Sarai: "Trust me. Follow me." Even if you have no plans to relocate, what insights about following the Lord do you gain from these verses?

Deuteronomy 13:4 *serve him, trust in him, he will show the way.*

Psalm 16:8 focas on the Lord,
will bring place/confidence.
at Rt. hand → he will not be moved
Psalm 91:2 he is my refuge, place of
safety, I will trust him all
John 10:27 of my days

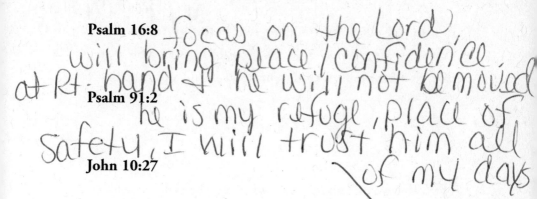

i. As recorded in **Genesis 12:2–3,** the Lord made seven promises to
Abram. Find each one, restating them to begin with "I will," since
all seven reflect God's future accomplishments, not Abram's future
efforts.

I will

I will

I will

I will

I will

I will

I will

How might such promises increase your faith in God?

very good chpt.

j. In light of God's vows to Abram, read **Psalm 91:14–16** and hear them as very much directed toward *you*. According to this passage, what prompts God to make such generous promises to his people?

For your own encouragement, write out the eight "I will" statements the Lord makes in this passage, replacing "him" with "you."

I will *deliver you*

I will *set you on high*

I will *call upon you*

I will *answer you*

I will *be with you in trouble*

I will *honor you*

I will *satisfy you*

I will *show you salvation*

All of history affirms the wisdom of following God.

Liz Curtis Higgs in *Slightly Bad Girls of the Bible*, page 16

4a. **Genesis 12:11** tells us that Sarai was a beautiful woman. In what way did that alter your perception of her?

b. When you first read **Genesis 12:14–15,** did you fear for Sarai in Pharaoh's court or assume her pleasing appearance would protect her?

c. In our culture how is beauty an advantage? A disadvantage?

d. On page 21 of *Slightly Bad Girls of the Bible,* I wrote, "Ask Bathsheba or Dinah or Tamar, the sister of Absalom, how beauty can lead to tragedy." So…let's ask them. Read the following passages and note what happened to each woman.

Bathsheba in **2 Samuel 11:2–4:**

Dinah in **Genesis 34:1–2:**

Tamar in **2 Samuel 13:1–2, 14:**

e. In all three instances, who was clearly to blame? And who was innocent?

f. How might such stories speak to women today who've been un-justly accused of "asking for it" simply because they're attractive?

g. What does **Proverbs 31:30** tell us about beauty? In what specific ways have you discovered that to be true in your life?

The Bible mentions a woman's appearance only when her story hinges on that fact. What the Lord applauds in his Word is a woman's character.

Liz Curtis Higgs in *Slightly Bad Girls of the Bible,* page 22

5a. In **Genesis 15:4** God told Abram he would father a son from his own seed but did not mention the mother's name. How might the story have unfolded differently if God had said here, "And Sarai will bear this son"?

b. To our human way of thinking, it may seem that the Lord erred in keeping this important detail to himself. But what do the following verses tell us about God?

Deuteronomy 32:4

2 Samuel 22:31

Isaiah 25:1

c. Why do you think God withheld this vital fact from Abram? Read the following passages and note one recurring theme, which may help answer this question.

Ecclesiastes 7:8

Hebrews 6:12–15

Romans 12:12

d. **Genesis 15:6** is a key verse for understanding God's grace. Below, write out the words of this verse, then ponder them for a moment.

In a nutshell, what did Abram do? And what did God do?

How does this verse apply to your relationship with God?

e. The impact of Abram's decision is mentioned in the New Testament no less than five times. Read the following passages and note how we're related to Father Abraham and what that means.

Galatians 3:29

Romans 4:23–24

Luke 19:9–10

f. As for Mother Sarai, **Genesis 16:3** tells us that Abram and Sarai had been living in Canaan ten years before she took steps to secure an heir for her husband. Why do you think she waited so long? What do you suppose finally prompted her to act?

Do you think Sarai arrived at the same place as our fictional Sandi: "she wasn't convinced God cared enough to intervene"? Why or why not?

g. How does **Psalm 106:13** apply to Sarai's situation?

> When it comes to timing, no chronometer on earth is the equal of God's stopwatch.
>
> Liz Curtis Higgs in *Slightly Bad Girls of the Bible*, page 22

6a. In **Genesis 16:3** we're told Sarai "took" and "gave" Hagar to her husband. How might her actions have led to a spiritual catastrophe in this household of faith?

b. Read **Isaiah 47:10–11** for a vivid description of a catastrophe and note what kind of thinking brings it on.

c. Was Sarai's solution—sanctioned by local custom—reasonable from a human standpoint? What makes you say that?

d. What contrasts do **Proverbs 12:15, Proverbs 16:1,** and **Proverbs 16:25** highlight between human solutions and divine ones?

e. What instruction for dealing with frustration or disappointment does **James 5:16** offer, and how might that apply to Sarai?

f. In what ways did Hagar's quick conception make matters worse for Sarai? **Proverbs 19:10** and **Psalm 13:2** touch on some possible answers.

g. On pages 31–32 of *Slightly Bad Girls of the Bible,* I refer to "poor Sarai" and "poor Hagar" as dual victims of a social system that honored their wombs, not their womanhood. Do you agree? If you sympathize with only one of these women, which one, and why?

h. Describe a time when you took your future into your own impatient hands without seeking God's guidance. What was the outcome?

Psalm 27:14 is a great verse to tuck in your memory bank for just such times. What, if anything, are you waiting for now? And what would it look like for you to "wait" and "be strong" and "take heart"?

> Only when we realize God is in control can we truly let go
> of our apprehensions.
>
> Liz Curtis Higgs in *Slightly Bad Girls of the Bible,* page 24

7a. **Genesis 16:5** reads like a closing argument in a jury trial. Note
each statement in Sarai's tersely presented prosecution.

Of Abram she says:

Of herself Sarai says:

Of Hagar she says:

Of the Lord she says:

b. Read **1 Samuel 24:12** and **Lamentations 3:59,** then describe the
"wrong" Sarai was suffering.

c. Was Hagar's treatment of Sarai a sin? What do **Romans 12:3** and
Romans 14:10 suggest?

d. When have you (be honest) looked down on someone—even in
passing—because of appearance, education, social status, or anything else that made that person "less than" in your eyes? In light
of **1 Peter 3:8,** what will you resolve to do in the future?

e. Once again, Sarai did not turn to the Lord for help. What reason would you offer?

f. Neither Abram nor Sarai behaved admirably in this chapter. Why do you suppose God chooses to bless such flawed people? What answers do **Micah 7:18–20** and **1 Timothy 1:15–16** suggest?

g. This chapter of Sarai's life ended on a distressing note. Have you lost respect for her, or are you willing to give her another chance? Explain why.

> Sarai was human, just as we are, and, as such, her story gives us hope.
>
> Liz Curtis Higgs in *Slightly Bad Girls of the Bible*, page 36

8. What's the most important lesson you learned from Sarai, a princess bride who ran out of patience?

2

Flight Plan

Hagar

Who *was* this exotic Egyptian woman, this handmaid of Sarai, who played such a pivotal role in the life of Abram? I confess, at the start of my research, I knew far less about Hagar than our other Slightly Bad Girls. With each new discovery, I grew more wide eyed. She did *that*? And said *what*? Her distinctly different yet parallel visits to the desert made my storyteller's heart beat faster, while her biblical firsts deserve proper recognition. Let's hear it for Hagar, a woman full of surprises.

1a. The Bible introduces Hagar in **Genesis 16:1,** disclosing three vital facts. What are they, and why does each one matter as her story unfolds?

b. How acquainted were you with Hagar's story before reading *Slightly Bad Girls of the Bible*? Did you expect to like or dislike her, and why? How has your opinion about her changed, if at all?

c. The Word of God features dozens of stories about unnamed women, yet this servant of Sarai is very much named. As noted on page 47 of *Slightly Bad Girls of the Bible,* what does Hagar's name mean? In what ways does that name suit her?

d. Scripture discloses not only Hagar's name but also her personality, revealed through her behavior. Read each of the following verses, then note under the appropriate category the character trait the verse suggests. For example, her *insolence* (verse 4) made her a Slightly Bad Girl; her eventual *obedience* to the angel's command (verse 9) made her a Mostly Good Girl.

	SLIGHTLY BAD GIRL	MOSTLY GOOD GIRL
Genesis 16:4		
Genesis 16:8		
Genesis 16:9		
Genesis 16:13		
Genesis 16:15		
Genesis 21:19		
Genesis 21:21		

e. Which of Hagar's negative traits landed her in the most trouble? Which of her positive traits do you most admire, and why?

f. Pride often lurks beneath our less-than-lovely character traits, while humility lies at the heart of our pleasing ones. Contrast the consequences of pride and humility as described in the following verses.

Proverbs 3:34

Proverbs 11:2

Isaiah 5:15–16

g. Sarai's envy of Hagar—for the child she carried and the place she held in Abram's life—and Hagar's lack of sympathy for barren Sarai turned them both into Mean Girls of the Bible. When have you experienced or observed this kind of woman-to-woman cruelty?

What directives in **Luke 6:27–28** and **1 Thessalonians 5:15** can help us avoid such behavior?

On the day Hagar became Abram's secondary wife, everything changed—for better and for worse.

Liz Curtis Higgs in *Slightly Bad Girls of the Bible*, page 45

2a. Do you think Hagar was a Slightly Bad Girl for agreeing to sleep
with Abram? What other choices would a slave have had in her
time and place?

b. It's quite possible Hagar delighted in her new role as her master's
secondary wife. What practical benefits might she have enjoyed?

c. Once they were husband and wife, how might Hagar's attitude
toward Abram have changed? Our fictional Pavla realized that car-
rying Alan's son had created a bond between them. Do you suppose
Hagar would have felt the same connection with Abram? Why or
why not?

d. Think of a recent situation in your life when you felt compelled to
do something, even though you didn't agree with it, simply because
that behavior is deemed acceptable in our culture. How did you
handle things, and what was the outcome?

e. When God's Word says one thing and society says another, how
can we find the strength to stand up for what we believe? See what
encouragement you find in the following verses.

Galatians 1:10

Matthew 10:22

Psalm 118:6

> Much as she wins our sympathy, legally Hagar was in the
> wrong.
>
> Liz Curtis Higgs in *Slightly Bad Girls of the Bible*, page 47

3a. In **Genesis 16:7** the angel of the Lord makes his scriptural debut,
appearing to Hagar—a woman, an Egyptian, a slave. Amazing, eh?
This was a foreshadowing of a new day, described in **Galatians
3:28.** Note the difference Christ makes.

Now meet the recipients of other such visitations from the angel of
the Lord. For each of the following passages, note the individual's
name, what the Lord said, and how the person responded.

Genesis 22:11

Exodus 3:2–4

Judges 6:12, 22

b. You'll note in the verses we just read that the angel of the Lord "called out" or "appeared." But in **Genesis 16:7,** he didn't just show up; he *found* Hagar, which suggests he was seeking her out. What else do we learn about the angel of the Lord in **Psalm 34:7,** and how does that description apply to Hagar's situation?

c. When the angel of the Lord first spoke to her, Hagar didn't shake in her sandals or tremble in her tunic. Based on the following verses, make a note of how people *usually* react when God shows up.

Jeremiah 5:22

Luke 2:9

Why might Hagar have responded differently? How do you think *you* would react if the angel of the Lord came looking for you?

d. In **Genesis 16:8** Hagar answered one of the angel's two questions. Do you hear defiance in her response or a confession of her sin? Why do you think she didn't answer his question about where she was going?

e. Have you ever been so overwhelmed or upset that you rushed away from a situation without a destination in mind? Where did you land? What did you discover about yourself?

f. When the angel commanded Hagar to go back to Sarai, she didn't protest despite the pain that might await her. How would you explain Hagar's willingness to obey his angelic order?

What do **Leviticus 25:18** and **Psalm 119:60** teach us about the best way to respond to God's instructions?

g. As you review **Genesis 16:9–12,** you'll notice that Hagar fell silent. Perhaps Hagar suddenly realized who was speaking! According to **Proverbs 17:28,** what are some benefits of remaining silent?

h. Though the Scriptures do not tell us "And Hagar went back," we know she did. If the Lord has ever compelled you to return to a trying situation, what was the outcome? How did you grow as a result of your obedience?

What encouragement does **1 Peter 1:6–7** offer us in the midst of such a trial?

Accepting God's existence is one thing; honoring his command is another matter entirely.

Liz Curtis Higgs in *Slightly Bad Girls of the Bible,* page 49

4a. Hagar showed great confidence in naming the One who visited her in the desert *El Roi*—pronounced "el-roh-ee" rather than like "Elroy" on *The Jetsons*! Was her naming of God a sacrilegious act, or was it worship? What insight does **Psalm 29:2** bring to that question?

b. Of course *El Roi* is only one of the Lord's many names. In **Psalm 113:2–3** what does David tell us we are to do with the name of the Lord?

c. One familiar name for the Lord appears in **Exodus 3:15.** What is that very long name, and what does God himself say about this name to Moses?

d. See how many additional names or attributes of the Lord you can
   think of. To prompt your memory, try making a list from A to Z.
   Here's how I got around the tricky ones: Q is "Quickening Spirit"
   (1 Corinthians 15:45, KJV), X is "eXcellent" (Psalm 148:13, KJV),
   and Z is "Zion's Cornerstone" (Isaiah 28:16).

A	J	S
B	K	T
C	L	U
D	M	V
E	N	W
F	O	X
G	P	Y
H	Q	Z
I	R	

e. Hagar's chosen name for the Lord, "God Who Sees Me," has such
   a personal meaning. What would you name God, and why?

f. Do you believe God also sees you? Hears you? Loves you? On what
   do you base your beliefs?

   How might these passages increase your confidence in a God
   who sees and hears?

   Psalm 33:13–15

   1 John 5:14

g. On page 52 of *Slightly Bad Girls of the Bible,* I observe, "Not only did God see Hagar; *she saw God,*" a most unusual experience. When the parents of Samson realized their visitor was the angel of the Lord, they were shocked. What did they say, according to **Judges 13:22?**

Why did Hagar seem unconcerned about such an outcome? How might the response of Samson's mom in **Judges 13:23** sum things up?

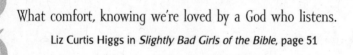

What comfort, knowing we're loved by a God who listens.
Liz Curtis Higgs in *Slightly Bad Girls of the Bible,* page 51

5a. Moving forward in Hagar's life, we find Ishmael in his teens and Abraham's younger son, Isaac, in toddlerhood. Read **Genesis 21:8–10,** then describe Abraham's feast on the day Isaac was weaned, as you picture it. What were the guests talking about? What foods do you suppose were served?

b. Read **Deuteronomy 16:14** and **Isaiah 25:6** and note the descriptions of what a fine feast *should* involve.

c. Have you ever been to a festive gathering where someone's presence left everyone on edge or a person's leaving brought the party back to life? Describe the situation, looking for similarities with Abraham's shindig.

Proverbs 22:10 offers wise advice, should a kill-joy like Ishmael show up. How could you follow this advice without resorting to Sarah's rude measures?

d. As you picture the teenager Ishmael mocking toddler Isaac, what words do you imagine Ishmael spoke, and what might have been his motive? Consider **James 4:1–3** for additional insight.

e. Do you think Hagar tried to prevent Ishmael's insubordinate behavior? Or might she have encouraged it and, if so, to what end?

What wisdom does **Proverbs 29:17** offer parents?

f. Whatever his flaws, Ishmael was destined to father a great nation, as we learned in **Genesis 16:10** and **Genesis 21:18.** We also know from Scripture that God doesn't condone mocking—see **Proverbs 19:29** and **Isaiah 29:20** for proof—yet he remained with Ishmael through manhood. What explanation would you offer for this?

> The first woman in Scripture to be given a divine promise of descendants was Hagar, the headstrong slave.
>
> Liz Curtis Higgs in *Slightly Bad Girls of the Bible*, page 50

6a. Twice Hagar found herself in what **Jeremiah 2:6** describes as "a land of deserts and rifts, a land of drought and darkness, a land where no one travels and no one lives." Sounds pretty bleak. What's the significance of Hagar's wandering in a desert rather than through a forest or a meadow?

b. **Psalm 63:1** and **Psalm 107:4–6** capture our despair when we find ourselves in a wasteland. If you've ever spent time in a spiritual wilderness, describe your experience.

c. For those difficult days, what assurance do we find in **Nehemiah 9:19** and **Deuteronomy 31:8?**

d. **Jeremiah 2:13** aptly addresses how *not* to solve the problem. In what ways did you perhaps forsake God during your desert season? And what "cisterns" did you dig in search of man-made solutions?

e. Consider the following passages. Note what each suggests about our need and God's provision.

	OUR NEED	GOD'S PROVISION
Isaiah 41:17–18		
John 4:13–14		

f. In what ways have you experienced God as a spring of living water that quenches your thirst?

g. As we read in **Genesis 21:19,** Hagar had a truly eye-opening experience in the desert. What do **Numbers 22:31, Mark 8:25,** and **Luke 24:30–31** teach us about *why* God opens the eyes of his people?

When has the Lord opened your eyes to a truth you needed to see?

h. Think of women you've known whose difficult lives might parallel Hagar's in some way. Drawing on Hagar's experiences in the wilderness—or on your own—what encouragement could you offer them?

God knew Hagar's hurts just as he knows ours.

Liz Curtis Higgs in *Slightly Bad Girls of the Bible*, page 62

7a. Though Hagar may have felt abandoned by her master and mistress, God remained by her side and Ishmael's as well, according to **Genesis 21:20.** Each of the following verses names a godly man whom the Lord favored with his abiding love. Note each name beside the verse, along with the phrase from the passage that most encourages you.

Genesis 39:2

1 Samuel 3:19

1 Chronicles 28:20

b. Having God "with us" doesn't simply mean having a sense of well-being in our souls. We can also experience a tangible awareness of his presence. Considering the preceding passages, in what ways do you think God was "with the boy" Ishmael as he matured?

c. In **Joshua 1:8–9** how did the Lord instruct his prophet to take him with him, as it were? And how, practically speaking, can you do the same?

d. In **Acts 10:37–38** we get an even clearer view of what it means to have God "with us" by seeing what his Son accomplished during his time on earth. In what specific ways might you, too, go around doing good because God is with you?

e. How do you explain God's loving care of Hagar and her son when Ishmael was not the one through whom Abraham's blessing would flow?

That God cares for *any* of us, flawed as we are, is remarkable, as **Psalm 144:3** suggests. Read **Psalm 145:17** and note its tender explanation.

f. Is it necessary to fully understand God's ways before you put your faith in him? What further insight do you gain from **Isaiah 55:8–9**?

g. What *must* you know about God to trust him as Hagar did? See if **Isaiah 45:5–6** helps you answer this question.

Write this on the tablet of your heart, beloved: God keeps his word.

Liz Curtis Higgs in *Slightly Bad Girls of the Bible*, page 50

8. What's the most important lesson you learned from Hagar, who beat a path to the desert twice and found God waiting for her both times?

3

The Last Laugh

Sarah

I know, I know: Sarai hardly deserves another chapter after mistreating, then expelling, Hagar. Thank goodness we love and serve a God of second chances. (If my own life is any indication, he is also a God of *forty-second* chances.) Let's reconnect with our matriarch just in time to watch her get a new name and have a good laugh. No joke! The words *laugh,* *laughter,* and *laughed* appear a perfect seven times in the NIV translation of this story. It's grand to know the Lord has a sublime sense of humor. And a breathtaking way of keeping his promises.

1a. Many of us have altered our first names over the years: *Missy* through high school, *Melissa* through law school; *Annabelle* printed on the birth certificate, *Belle* engraved on the wedding napkins. If you've had a name change, first or last, describe the experience. Did you find it bothersome, as our fictional Sandra did, to keep correcting people? Or did you hear your new name as a welcome reminder of a new chapter in your life?

b. Though we see little difference between the names *Sarai* and *Sarah,* the distinction mattered to God. In **Genesis 17:15** he marked her new identity as one in covenant with him just as he marked Abraham's body through circumcision, as described in **Genesis 17:11.**

According to **Genesis 17:16,** what role did God give Sarah in his everlasting covenant?

c. Her new title sounds daunting. Yet all of us—single or married, with or without children—mother the next generation. Consider the following areas of your influence, with biblical guidance included. In what ways will the life you live today affect the future of each one?

Your family: **Acts 10:2; 1 Timothy 5:8**

Our society: **Luke 10:36–37; Romans 13:10**

God's creation: **Genesis 1:26; Romans 8:19–21**

God's kingdom: **Colossians 3:23–24; Ephesians 3:7–9**

d. Consider Paul's words to Timothy about his spiritual lineage in
    2 Timothy 1:5. How does Timothy's foundation compare with
    your own experience? What spiritual heritage can you claim, as
    David did in **Psalm 61:5** or as Paul described in **Acts 20:32**?

e. If you're a first-generation believer, what assurance of your spiritual
    inheritance does **Ephesians 1:13–14** offer you?

f. Perhaps the most thrilling way of becoming a "mother of nations"
    is sharing in the birth of new believers, nurturing them in the faith,
    and helping them reach maturity. What encouragement do you
    find in the following verses, and how can you act on it?

    1 Thessalonians 2:8

    1 Peter 2:2–3

    Ephesians 4:11–15

Here's the *truly* exciting part: God irrevocably included
Sarah in his promises to Abraham.

Liz Curtis Higgs in *Slightly Bad Girls of the Bible*, page 76

2a. Abraham laughed to himself when God promised to give him a son by Sarah. In what ways do **Job 8:21, Psalm 19:8,** and **Psalm 126:2** capture the heart of his response?

What other reasons might have prompted Abraham to laugh?

b. God did not ask Abraham, "Why did you laugh?" but he did ask Sarah. What explanation could you offer for God accepting Abraham's amusement but not Sarah's?

c. Perhaps the following verses help explain the difference between Abraham's laughter and Sarah's. Note the insight each offers concerning faith (or the lack of it) and God's faithfulness.

Hebrews 11:6

Psalm 78:38

2 Corinthians 4:16

d. Jesus was laughed at too and very publicly. Read **Matthew 9:23–26,** then answer the following questions.

What was Jesus' mission here?

Who laughed at him and why?

Was he dissuaded by their laughter?

What did he do next?

And what was the outcome?

e. Have you, like Sarah, ever laughed at God out of disbelief? Perhaps scoffed at a promise made in Scripture, certain it won't happen in *your* life? What does such laughter reveal about us?

How can we replace the laughter of doubt with the joy of faith?

f. Though the Lord surely has a sense of humor (giraffes, llamas, and platypuses are living proof), you may be surprised to discover what amuses him. Read the following verses to determine whom God laughs at and why.

Psalm 2:2–4

Psalm 37:12–13

Proverbs 1:22–27

g. Does this image of God mocking man's foolishness disturb you?
Why or why not?

How might **Romans 3:3–4** put your mind at ease?

h. Sarah was not alone in her unbelief. Read **Luke 1:11–20** to find
out what happened when the angel of the Lord appeared to
Zechariah, then compare the following two verses, noting what
Zechariah and Sarah had in common.

Luke 1:18

Genesis 18:12

We find in **Luke 1:20** that hapless Zechariah not only didn't
laugh; he couldn't speak! For what purpose do you think the angel
afflicted him?

Read **Luke 1:59–65** for this story's happy ending. Verses 64 and 65
help us understand the reason for Zechariah's silent treatment.
What did the new father do? And what did his neighbors do?

> Just as God knew how to deal with Sarah's doubt, he can handle ours.
>
> Liz Curtis Higgs in *Slightly Bad Girls of the Bible*, page 84

3a. In *Daughters of Eve*, author Virginia Stem Owens suggested, "Instead of Sarah the Faithful, she could as easily be called Sarah the Scornful or Sarah the Spiteful." Do those words—*scornful* and *spiteful*—provide a fair assessment of Sarah? Why or why not?

b. Taking into account the whole of her life, what descriptive word(s) would you assign to Sarah, and why?

c. What makes us grow spiritually, and why? Is it worshiping with others? Reading Christian books? Doing good deeds? Being with others who are like-minded? Or do we grow most through adversity? What does **James 1:2–4** suggest?

d. What does **1 Corinthians 3:6–7** tell us about spiritual growth? What is God's role, and what is ours?

e. How did God "grow" Sarah?

Consider **2 Thessalonians 1:3–5,** then describe how God has "grown" you in the past six months.

f. If your friends were to assign you a telling title that reflects your faith—Susan the Brave or Kathy the Timid—what words might they choose, and why?

> The Lord knows everything we think, say, and do, yet abides with us still. And blesses us in spite of ourselves.
>
> Liz Curtis Higgs in *Slightly Bad Girls of the Bible*, page 86

4a. On page 79 of *Slightly Bad Girls of the Bible,* I raise the question, did Abraham inform Sarah about God's promise that she would give birth to Abraham's heir? Then on page 82 I offered three reasons why I think her husband didn't tell her. Which of those ring true to you, and why?

What other option(s) can you suggest?

b. If Abraham *did* withhold this vital news from Sarah, what might have been his motive?

c. Why might Sarah have benefited from hearing the news directly from God rather than from her husband?

d. Which has more impact on you: hearing a minister or teacher proclaim a vital truth *or* discovering that same truth in the Bible on your own? Why?

e. Note all the dynamic ways the voice of the Lord is described in **Psalm 29.**

Verse 3

Verse 4

Verse 5

Verse 7

Verse 8

Verse 9

Contrast this with how the Lord's voice is described in **1 Kings 19:12** and **Job 4:15–16.**

f. It's not the volume of God's voice but the words themselves that hold the power to change us. Have you ever had a sense that God was speaking directly to your heart? If so, did he speak in a thunder or a whisper? And what did he tell you?

g. You'll recall that our fictional Sandra was skeptical about her ability to bear a child, even when Rev. Theo Finney (how could I resist playing off *theophany*?!) assured her, "Your age, madam, is of no concern to God." How can we know we've heard from the Lord and not merely from a person? See if **1 Thessalonians 5:19–21** offers a helpful perspective.

> Sarah needed to hear this promise with her own ears.
>
> Liz Curtis Higgs in *Slightly Bad Girls of the Bible*, page 81

5a. As **Joshua 23:14** and **2 Corinthians 1:20** affirm, a promise or prophecy fulfilled in Scripture builds our faith in a God who keeps his word. What does **2 Peter 1:20–21** reveal about prophecy in the Bible?

And what does **Revelation 1:3** suggest our response to biblical prophecy should be?

b. When Sarah bore a son to Abraham "at the very time God had promised him" (**Genesis 21:2**), how do you suppose that prophetic fulfillment changed her relationship with her husband? And with her God?

c. How might Abraham's actions noted in **Genesis 21:3–5** demonstrate his faith in the Lord, especially in light of his age?

d. How did Sarah express her faith in God in **Genesis 21:6–7**?

e. Perhaps the greatest promise in God's Word can be found in **Romans 10:9.** Take a moment to write out this short verse, letting the truth of each phrase sink in. How does this verse build your faith?

f. **Acts 2:39** tells us for whom that promise is meant. Have you embraced that truth from Romans for yourself? If so, describe your initial experience and how it has affected your life since.

g. Even those who believe in God can stumble. When Sarah evicted Hagar and Ishmael, was that a loss of faith on Sarah's part or a necessary step for everyone involved? Explain your answer.

h. Note how each key player suffered from the permanent separation…and how each benefited.

	How Each Suffered	How Each Benefited
Abraham		
Sarah		
Isaac		
Hagar		
Ishmael		

How might **Romans 8:28** apply to this situation?

> Sarah may have laughed at God's promise, but she was the
> first to praise him when that promise was fulfilled.
>
> Liz Curtis Higgs in *Slightly Bad Girls of the Bible*, page 89

6a. We didn't study Abraham's later willingness to sacrifice Isaac on
   Mount Moriah because it fell outside the parameters of Sarah's
   story. But she was very much alive when it happened. Read
   Genesis 22:1–19 for this moving account. What was evident
   about Abraham's faith right from **verse 1**?

  b. What word(s) would you use to describe God's request in **Genesis
   22:2**? And what would *your* immediate response have been?

  c. What was Abraham's response, as described in **Genesis 22:3**? How
   would you account for his behavior?

  d. In **Genesis 22:5** what did Abraham tell his servants he and Isaac
   were going to do? Was he hiding the truth from them…or revealing
   it? Explain your answer.

e. In some ways Isaac foreshadows the Messiah: a son, miraculously conceived, who carried the wood on his back for his own impending sacrifice. When Isaac asked his father about the lamb, what was Abraham's answer in **Genesis 22:8**? And what does the rest of the verse indicate about Isaac's *and* Abraham's faith in God?

f. Do you see any hesitancy, any second thoughts reflected in Abraham's actions in **Genesis 22:9–10**?

g. How do **Hebrews 11:17–19** and **James 2:21–23** explain such unwavering faith?

h. Now let's consider Sarah's involvement. Do you imagine she knew about Abraham's intentions when he left with Isaac that day? What makes you say that?

i. How might a mother handle such a request from God differently than a father would?

j. How can we trust a God who would require such a sacrifice? Jot down any phrases or insights from the following verses that help you answer this challenging question.

1 John 4:10

Romans 3:25–26

Ephesians 5:1–2

Hebrews 9:27–28

> God's compassion for Slightly Bad Girls like Sarah—like us—knows no bounds.
>
> Liz Curtis Higgs in *Slightly Bad Girls of the Bible*, page 87

7a. How would you characterize Abraham and Sarah's marriage relationship? Adversarial or companionable? Distant or intimate? Would **Ephesians 5:33** describe them?

And how did their relationship change over the years?

b. Which spouse seemed to have the stronger personality? Explain your answer.

c. How do **Proverbs 5:18** and **Proverbs 31:23** suit Abraham? What did you respect about Abraham as a husband? And what did you find difficult to accept about him?

d. As for Sarah, the Bible tells us in **Proverbs 19:14** that "a prudent wife is from the LORD." In what ways was Sarah indeed prudent, meaning "wise and careful"?

e. Prudence is a virtue for any woman, married or single. In what ways do you fit that description? And what area(s) of your life might benefit from more wisdom and diligence?

f. In **Titus 2:3–5** we find a list of expectations for older women, including skills meant to be taught to younger women. How would Sarah do as a Titus 2 woman? Make a list based on the passage in Titus (I found ten "commandments" in all), then circle those qualities you've seen at work in Sarah's life.

(1)

(2)

(3)

(4)

(5)

(6)

(7)

(8)

(9)

(10)

As you look over this list, underline any characteristics you may need to work on.

g. Read again Abraham's response to Sarah's death in **Genesis 23:2.** What does his grieving tell us about their years together?

Not only did God bless Sarah; so did her husband to the very end.

Liz Curtis Higgs in *Slightly Bad Girls of the Bible*, page 89

8. What's the most important lesson you learned from Sarah, a woman who laughed at God and (almost) got away with it?

4

A Willful Bride

Rebekah the Wife

N ever has a biblical love story started on a sweeter note. Obedient Abraham sent a trustworthy servant to find Isaac a bride, who turned out to
be beautiful, generous, and chaste. Rebekah comforted her new husband,
and Isaac loved his new wife. Why, oh why can't we end this tale on that
happy crescendo? Because, as we all know, life is seldom that simple, and
humans are never far from sin. Let's walk beside Rebekah in tandem with
Isaac, seeing what God might want to teach us about our shared strengths…
and weaknesses.

1a. According to **Genesis 35:28,** Isaac lived one hundred and eighty
years, so he was still relatively young when he married at forty. On
page 109 of *Slightly Bad Girls of the Bible,* how is Isaac described?
Are those attributes in a man generally celebrated in our culture?
Why might that be the case?

b. What about in Scripture? Are mellow, meditative men applauded
there? Note what David, Job, Solomon, and Amos said about such
qualities.

Psalm 119:148

Job 6:24

Ecclesiastes 9:17

Amos 5:13

c. If you have an Isaac in your life who struggles because he's not a hard-driving, outspoken, macho kind of guy, how could you encourage him emotionally and spiritually?

d. What incidents in Isaac's early years might have shaped his laid-back personality? **Genesis 21:5** and **Genesis 22:9–10** offer two clues.

e. No matter his age, a man who loves his mother grieves her passing. In what ways might go-go Rebekah have reminded Isaac of his mother?

f. Do you think **Proverbs 27:15–16** captures Isaac's life with Rebekah…or might that scenario better suit Abraham and Sarah? Explain your choice.

If you are a quarrelsome woman, how might you restrain yourself?

g. What are the pluses of marrying someone who is your opposite? What are the minuses?

h. Since we know the Lord chose Rebekah for Isaac, list some possible reasons God viewed this as a perfect match.

Abraham was a man of action, but his son Isaac was a man of prayer.

Liz Curtis Higgs in *Slightly Bad Girls of the Bible*, page 112

2a. Abraham's servant remains nameless in Genesis 24, from first verse to last. How is his role in Abraham's household described in **Genesis 24:2**?

He sounds quite important. Since "a righteous man will be remembered forever" (**Psalm 112:6**), could it be that our deeds will be venerated rather than our names? How would you prefer to be remembered, and why?

b. If he *was* Eliezer, the man slated to inherit all of Abraham's wealth
had there been no heir, then finding a wife for Isaac was a supreme
act of loyalty on his part. What other words would you use to
describe this servant, based on his words and actions detailed in the
following verses, and the attributes—humility, patience, wisdom—
they display?

	HIS WORDS AND ACTIONS	HIS ATTRIBUTES
Genesis 24:9		
Genesis 24:12		
Genesis 24:26–27		
Genesis 24:33		
Genesis 24:49		
Genesis 24:56		

c. Think of someone you know who exhibits all those commendable
qualities, the sort of person described in **Psalm 37:30.** Would
you completely entrust the future happiness of someone you love
to such a person, without any involvement on your part? Why or
why not?

d. Would attaining that level of trust require you to have more faith in the person—or greater faith in God? Explain your answer.

e. The servant asked God for a specific sign—"If that happens, I will know she is the right one" (**Genesis 24:14,** ICB)—thinking a woman willing to go the extra mile would make a good wife for Isaac. Did asking for a sign mean the servant lacked faith, or was he simply seeking direction? What makes you say that?

What do **Judges 6:17** and **Psalm 86:17** suggest?

f. Signs of God at work also appear in the New Testament. In the following verses, we have evidence that the Lord Jesus performed miracles to build the faith of his first-century followers. For each verse below, note the outcome, which matters far more than the sign itself.

John 2:11

John 2:23

John 3:2

Offering to water ten thirsty camels? That would take a
miracle of God and one very benevolent young woman.

Liz Curtis Higgs in *Slightly Bad Girls of the Bible*, page 99

3a. According to **Genesis 24:19–20,** Rebekah *did* go the extra mile
(and a zillion extra steps!) to water the servant's ten camels. How
would you explain her benevolent effort? Youthful enthusiasm?
Heartfelt generosity? A prompting from the Lord?

b. Speaking of steps, Rebekah not only flew up and down them physically; she was also walking metaphorically on a path chosen by
God. What do the following verses affirm about her actions? And
what do they mean for your life?

Psalm 37:23–24

Psalm 85:13

Proverbs 16:9

c. How does Rebekah's story confirm the principle described in
Psalm 112:5?

d. Or could Rebekah's motivation have been less than altruistic? To impress the men? To earn a fistful of coins? To shame the other women who were watching? Why does a more negative motive seem unlikely here?

e. Of this we can be sure: Rebekah's water-bearing efforts were not what garnered the Lord's favor. Note the reasons God delights in a person, as described in **Psalm 147:10–11.**

f. Read **1 Peter 4:9,** then think of a recent incident when you were exceedingly generous or hospitable. What were your underlying motives?

How might **Proverbs 16:2** change your assessment of your actions?

What sense of confirmation from the Lord—a "Well done, good and faithful servant!" (**Matthew 25:21**)—did you receive?

And other than a happy recipient, what was the outcome of your altruistic deed?

Rebekah knew neither his identity nor his mission. Her
offer seems borne of a generous heart.

Liz Curtis Higgs in *Slightly Bad Girls of the Bible*, page 101

4a. Describe how you envision Rebekah's conversation, her facial
expressions, and her body language when she hurried to tell her
mother's household (**Genesis 24:28**).

b. Do you see any hint of the character flaws that surfaced later in her
life? Her impulsive nature perhaps? Anything else?

c. When we see and hear Rebekah's brother, Laban, in action in **Genesis 24:30–31,** his words ring false because of his overt interest
in the servant's many camels—and Rebekah's jewelry. Read the
warning in **1 Corinthians 15:33.** Do you see any indication that
Laban's nature corrupted Rebekah? What traits, if any, do she and
Laban appear to have in common?

d. Compare your younger self to the woman you are today. As a young woman, would your family and friends have described you as the servant did Rebekah—"The girl was very beautiful" (**Genesis 24:16**)—or as the young bridegroom did his bride in **Song of Songs 4:7**? What words do loved ones use to describe you now?

e. What of your character as a young woman? Were you innocent, like our Rebekah of **Genesis 24:16**? Or did you, like me, resemble a **Proverbs 7:10–12** woman? Whatever your past, how does **Psalm 103:11–12** assure you of God's love and forgiveness?

f. Read **Job 12:12.** How has your character changed for the better over the years? And in what ways have your flaws gained ground?

Strong-willed women can learn much from Rebekah—both what to do and what *not* to do.

Liz Curtis Higgs in *Slightly Bad Girls of the Bible*, page 120

5a. Rebekah's courageous statement "I will go" (**Genesis 24:58**) echoed
Abram's actions a generation earlier: "So Abram left, as the LORD
had told him" (**Genesis 12:4**). What other similarities between
Abraham and his future daughter-in-law—either in temperament
or behavior—can you find?

b. **Hebrews 11:8** outlines God's plan for Abraham to follow him.
How do the following verses illuminate the concept of God's
calling?

Isaiah 30:21

Isaiah 41:4

c. In light of the verses you've just read, explain how Rebekah might
have seen her relocation to a distant land as a calling from God.

d. We sense no hesitation in Rebekah. Why did she seem so eager to
leave? Was it the servant's godly manner? Her own bold personality?
Those lovely gifts? The family connection? The wealth to come?
Make a case for whatever explanation you find most compelling.

e. We're told in **Genesis 24:59–61** that several members of Rebekah's household accompanied her. Those who remained behind did something rather remarkable for a culture that placed little value on women. What did they do, and what did it signify? Did the words they spoke come to pass? Explain.

f. How would having family and friends along for the camel ride make such a venture easier for you? Or would you rather take off solo?

What would convince you that such a journey was God's idea and not yours? What counsel do you find in **Hebrews 3:1**?

g. Perhaps, on faith alone, you've launched down an uncertain path much as Rebekah did. Compare your experiences, briefly noting the specific details in your life.

	REBEKAH	YOU
Human invitation		
Divine calling		
Confirmation from others		

REBEKAH   YOU

Support of parents

Conferring of gifts

Farewell blessing

Moving forward

h. What lessons did you learn on your journey that have served you well to this day?

> Rebekah fearlessly left everything she knew to marry a man she'd never met.
>
> Liz Curtis Higgs in *Slightly Bad Girls of the Bible*, page 108

6a. Since no biblical description of Rebekah's long trek exists, we may conclude that the Lord was as eager for her to meet Isaac as we were. Yet we have no recorded conversation between the betrothed parties on that enchanted evening when Isaac and Rebekah first gazed at each other across a crowded field of camels. Why not, do you suppose?

b. After reading afresh the account of this long-anticipated meeting in **Genesis 24:63–66,** make a note of what each participant said and/or did.

	SAID	**DID**
Isaac		
Rebekah		
Servant		

Camels (just kidding…)

Who was the most active player in this scene? And the most passive? What clues about their pending marriage relationship do you find in this scene?

c. However reticent his personality, Isaac wasted no time in marrying Rebekah, as we read in **Genesis 24:67.** Would you have been ready to marry at once, as Rebekah was, or would you have insisted on a courtship of a certain length?

d. In what ways does Isaac exemplify the kind of love described in **Proverbs 20:6, Proverbs 21:21,** and **Psalm 85:10**?

e. Had strong-willed Sarah still been alive when bold and decisive Rebekah arrived in Canaan, how might that have changed the family dynamics?

f. Sarai's barren state comes up repeatedly in Scripture, yet Rebekah's twenty years of barrenness get only a passing mention. **Genesis 25:21** gives us a clue why that is the case.

g. What can we learn from each of the following passages about approaching God with our needs?

1 John 5:14–15

Matthew 7:7–11

John 16:24

h. Answered prayer builds our faith and gives us the courage to seek God again. In the last week what need(s), expressed in prayer, did God meet for you?

Take a moment now to pray for an unanswered need, then jot it down here with today's date, leaving space for a second date, when the Lord responds.

If we sincerely mean "Thy will be done," we may discover, as Isaac did, that our heart's desire and the Lord's are the same.

Liz Curtis Higgs in *Slightly Bad Girls of the Bible*, page 113

7a. Rebekah epitomized a woman on the move. With a battle raging in her womb, she went forth to "inquire of the LORD" (**Genesis 25:22**). To whom else might Rebekah have turned? If the Lord was her first resort, what does that tell us about her?

b. The first woman in the biblical record to give birth to twins, Rebekah understandably wanted to know the reason for her agony. God's response, found in **Genesis 25:23,** addressed both her present pain and her heartache to come. Was "the older will serve the younger" sufficient justification for Rebekah to love Jacob (and, it would seem, not love Esau)? Why or why not?

c. Though Esau was stronger physically, Jacob got the upper hand when Esau sold his birthright for a bowl of stew. As you read **Genesis 25:29–34,** which of Rebekah's sons do you find more at fault, and why?

d. Which aspects of Rebekah's personality do you recognize in Jacob? In Esau?

e. Does either son resemble his quiet, contemplative, praying father? How do you explain the traits you observe in their personalities?

f. God's Word offers good counsel for parents. What insights do you find in the following passages?

Proverbs 31:28–29

Colossians 3:18–21

Ephesians 6:4

g. If you have children, do you ever struggle with favoring one over the other(s)? What are some healthy ways to balance parental affection? Although **1 Corinthians 12:25–26** speaks of the family of God as a whole, how might that truth apply to your individual family as well?

h. Rebekah seemed to believe she was doing God's will by honoring Jacob over Esau. Does that make her a Slightly Bad Girl in your eyes…or simply an overzealous mother?

Rebekah had already made up her mind: whoever was born second would have her undivided attention.

Liz Curtis Higgs in *Slightly Bad Girls of the Bible*, page 119

8. What's the most important lesson you learned from our visit with Rebekah, a young wife who said "I will" with gusto?

5

Using Her Wits

Rebekah the Mother

Before this chapter ends, the question "Does Rebekah qualify as a Slightly Bad Girl?" will be definitively answered. Was Rebekah as devious as Rosalind Seaver with her bucket of Angelo's chicken? She was. Yet *Really Bad Girls of the Bible* featured two women who were "Bad for a Good Reason," a qualifier that might apply to our Rebekah. She'd sought the Lord, and he'd spoken to her directly. I have no doubt Rebekah considered "the older will serve the younger" her mandate from God. But we twenty-first-century sisters have the whole of God's Word to consider, and it says to "conduct yourselves in a manner worthy of the gospel of Christ" (Philippians 1:27). By that measuring stick, I fear our Slightly Bad Rebekah falls short—as on many days do we. Let's see what her actions can teach us.

1a. Throughout this chapter two brothers seek their father's blessing, a practice God instituted with their grandfather Abraham. In the NIV translation, the words *bless* and *blessing* first appear in the same verse, **Genesis 12:2.** The point of a blessing, it seems, is to pass it on. How are we directed to do just that in **Luke 6:27–31**?

b. In **Genesis 49:28** we find that Jacob blessed his twelve sons, one by one. According to this verse, what characterized each blessing?

c. Different blessings for different sons—does that seem unjust to you? Note what each of the following passages reveals about God's blessing of us.

Isaiah 30:18

Jeremiah 9:23–24

Ephesians 1:3

d. In your family have your parents "blessed" you and your siblings similarly? Differently?

e. Did your mother or father launch you into the world with a formal blessing—offering a prayer on your behalf, serving a special meal, or presenting you with a family heirloom? If so, describe the blessing and the impact it had on your life, then and now.

f. It's perfectly biblical to ask for a blessing, as we see in **1 Chronicles 4:10.** If you didn't receive a parental blessing, how could that be remedied—if not by your parents, then by someone you esteem?

g. And if you are a parent, how could you bless your children now—whatever their ages—and what sort of response would you expect?

The blessing of one's father represented a verbal will, a spoken scepter, an invisible crown of words circling the son's brow.

Liz Curtis Higgs in *Slightly Bad Girls of the Bible*, page 130

2a. We sensed Rebekah's frustration building from the moment she overheard Isaac's plans to bless Esau, described in **Genesis 27:4.** She couldn't control the situation, but she *could* control Jacob and, through him, Isaac. The woman was so in control she was out of control! Read **Proverbs 25:28.** What "city" was Rebekah destroying?

What comparison can you make between her behavior and the principle described in **Proverbs 14:1**?

b. What have you observed about people with control issues—their motives, their methods, and their results? (Some of us don't have to look very far to find the answer!) And how would you describe their general outlook on life, despite all their efforts to control things?

c. In light of Rebekah's personality, how would you differentiate between the following words?

Control and manipulation

Confidence and arrogance

Determination and obsession

d. Who is truly in charge, according to **1 Samuel 2:2, Job 42:2,** and **Jeremiah 10:6**?

e. How does knowing he is ultimately in control affect your perspective on self-control?

Galatians 5:22–23 features self-control among a long tally of admirable qualities. Who produces such fruit?

f. What areas of your life might benefit from less control on your part and more control on the Holy Spirit's part?

g. According to **2 Peter 1:5–8,** what role does self-control play in God's work in our lives?

h. Think of specific people in your life who may be chafing under your controlling influence. Read **Psalm 19:12–14,** then take a moment to write out a prayer of confession, asking the Lord to heighten your sensitivity and to diminish your desire for control.

Control issues plagued each of our Slightly Bad Girls— Rebekah most of all.

Liz Curtis Higgs in *Slightly Bad Girls of the Bible,* page 131

3a. As you review **Genesis 27:5–10,** do you think Rebekah carefully conceived her deception of Isaac in advance or overheard her husband talking with Esau and made a sudden decision to intervene? How did you come to your conclusion?

b. From an ethical standpoint, does it matter whether Rebekah's approach was premeditated or spontaneous? What additional insight do you gain from **Genesis 4:7** and **Psalm 15:1–3?**

c. One theme runs through this deception scene. Restate that theme as found in **Genesis 27:8, Genesis 27:13,** and **Genesis 27:43.**

Under what circumstances might you hear or say this phrase at your house? And how do you feel about those words now?

d. What do **Job 15:5** and **Proverbs 10:19** tell us about the connection between words and sin?

e. If Rebekah's motive was to secure the blessing for Jacob because of God's prophetic word to her, what thoughts might have bolstered her view of herself as a Supremely Good Girl bent on a righteous cause?

f. Though Rebekah might have defended her motives as pure, we see otherwise. What do the following verses teach us about such thinking?

Job 14:4

Proverbs 20:9

Note that both of the preceding verses pose a question. Summarize the single answer that fits them.

g. Had Rebekah *not* taken matters into her own hands, what might have happened?

h. If you've ever tried to help God, what was the result?

What does **Acts 17:24–25** make clear about God's need for our help?

Rebekah's motives were clear, but they weren't pure.

Liz Curtis Higgs in *Slightly Bad Girls of the Bible*, page 133

4a. When Rebekah started in with her impersonate-your-brother scheme, we hoped future-patriarch Jacob might take a **Proverbs 6:35** stance…but he didn't. Based on what we've seen so far, describe the character of Jacob, both his strengths and his weaknesses.

b. Why did Jacob not refuse to do Rebekah's bidding from the start? Beyond the hairy man–smooth man dilemma, what concerns might have been on his mind?

c. How do you imagine Jacob justified his behavior? What did Jesus say in **Luke 16:15** about such self-deception?

d. What are we to think of a young man who so easily lied to his father? And of a mother who urged him to do so? Read **Isaiah 3:12, Psalm 62:10,** and **Psalm 34:13** for additional perspective, then share your thoughts on this deceptive duo.

e. Do you agree that "the LORD your God gave me success" (**Genesis 27:20**) was the worst of Jacob's seven lies? Explain your answer. What does **Zechariah 13:3** suggest about the seriousness of this offense?

f. How would you parent Jacob if he were *your* son? Would you go to any lengths, as Rebekah did, to help him get the blessing promised by God? Or would you teach him the virtues of trusting the Lord, perhaps embroidering **Psalm 34:14** on his T-shirts?

> In our hurry to solve the crisis of the hour, we often fail to
> consider the long-range consequences of our short-term
> solutions.
>
> Liz Curtis Higgs in *Slightly Bad Girls of the Bible*, page 144

5a. I kept waiting for Isaac to realize he was conversing with Jacob
rather than with Esau. You too? In **Genesis 27:21–27**—the verses
leading up to the blessing itself—we see four of Isaac's senses
engaged: touch, hearing, taste, smell. But Isaac's failing eyesight
(**Genesis 27:1**) and his reclining position (**Genesis 27:19**) made
accurate perceptions more difficult for him. Still, there's more at
work here than physical limitations. How else would you explain
Isaac's inability to discern—or accept—the truth?

b. As we see in **Leviticus 19:14,** Jacob's deception of his blind father
suggests a lack of reverence not only for his father but also for God.
On page 139 of *Slightly Bad Girls of the Bible,* I compared Jacob's
kiss to that of another biblical betrayer: Judas. Read **Genesis
27:26–27** and **Matthew 26:48–49.** In what ways are these pivotal
moments alike, and how are they distinctive?

c. **Genesis 27:30** indicates that as soon as Isaac blessed him, Jacob
took off without another word. Why the rush, do you think? And
where would you guess he was headed?

How might this scene have unfolded if Esau had arrived *before* the blessing was bestowed?

d. Judging by everything Rebekah said at the start of this scene, what do you imagine she said to Jacob afterward?

e. **Genesis 27:35** makes it clear that Isaac charged Jacob alone with the deception. Do you think Isaac was at all to blame for his misdirected blessing? Explain your answer.

f. Deceit and betrayal are cruel in any time and place. What do the following verses reveal about God's view of such behavior?

Proverbs 17:20

Leviticus 19:11

Joshua 9:22–23

Proverbs 24:28

g. Have you ever been deceived by someone you trusted? What did you think of that person—and of yourself—when the truth was revealed?

What wisdom does **Micah 7:5–7** impart that could have changed your experience?

How did that betrayal affect your ability to hope in the Lord, as this prophet did?

Though one man in Rebekah's life was blessed, two other men would bear the fallout of her favoritism.

Liz Curtis Higgs in *Slightly Bad Girls of the Bible*, page 140

6a. The phrase "weeping and gnashing of teeth" (**Matthew 8:12**) well suits the scene we find in **Genesis 27:32–38.** Esau's weeping was so memorable that people were still talking about it two thousand years later! In the New Testament we read, "He could bring about no change of mind, though he sought the blessing with tears" (**Hebrews 12:17**). Did you feel sympathetic toward Esau in this scene, or did he deserve to lose his inheritance? What makes you say that?

b. Was the blessing ever truly Esau's since God had ordained Jacob as heir to the promise? Review **Genesis 12:3, Genesis 25:23,** and **Genesis 27:28–29,** then consider **Psalm 33:12** before explaining your answer.

c. **Deuteronomy 7:6–9** shows us how and why God bestowed his blessing on Abraham's descendants through Jacob. Verse by verse, note the following:

God chose them…

Not because…

But because…

Finally, he promised…

How does that last verse—**Deuteronomy 7:9**—affirm that God's promise is a "covenant of love" for us too?

d. When Isaac offered Esau a backhanded blessing, he spoke authoritatively. Did Isaac's words come from his heart, or were they somehow directed by God? How did you come to that conclusion?

e. What insight does Balaam's experience in **Numbers 23:11–12** lend to Isaac's difficult position?

And what does **Exodus 4:10–12** demonstrate about God's speaking through his people?

f. After Jacob's departure, what might Rebekah's relationship with Esau have been like? Do you imagine her confessing the part she played in the deception, then asking his forgiveness? Why or why not?

g. If you've wronged a family member, even in a small way, how did you make amends?

In lesser incidents I've had people brush off my apology as unnecessary. But **Proverbs 14:9** suggests it *is* necessary to make amends. What in your experience illustrates the truth of that verse?

> I cringe when I look at the emotional carnage around this queen of control.
>
> Liz Curtis Higgs in *Slightly Bad Girls of the Bible,* page 143

7a. The saga continues in **Genesis 27:42–46.** In the space of a few verses, we find Rebekah controlling both Jacob *and* Isaac. First, Rebekah mapped out Jacob's life for him. What did she expect him to do?

Did Rebekah ask her son's opinion, give him a choice, or define a time line? Who could put up with such a parent?! And why *did* Jacob put up with Rebekah, would you say?

b. Without missing a beat, Rebekah turned her attention to Isaac. In **Genesis 27:46,** one complaint from this drama queen set her husband in motion. Again, why do you think Isaac succumbed to her manipulations?

c. Have you ever done such a thing on a smaller scale—perhaps helping a loved one embrace a decision you'd already made for him or her? Describe your handling of the situation.

Why did you think such machinations necessary at the time?
Were they effective—that is to say, did you get your way? What
long-term effect did this have on your relationship with the person involved?

d. What counsel does God's Word provide concerning such behavior?

Proverbs 21:8

1 Corinthians 3:18–20

Strong words for strong-willed women: "devious," "foolish,"
"crafty." *Ouch.* Recognizing—and regretting—our controlling
behavior is a start, but let's not stop there. What perspective does
2 Corinthians 7:10 offer?

e. Read **2 Corinthians 4:2** and note below its inventory of things
those who've encountered God's mercy are to do and *not* to do.

To-Do List   *Not*-to-Do List

f. How do you envision Rebekah's relationship with Isaac after Jacob left? Do you think Isaac knew about her involvement behind the scenes, or was her husband truly in the dark?

g. Rebekah's last recorded speech in **Genesis 27:46** is quite telling. In your translation, how many times did she refer to living and/or dying? What precisely did she say?

What significance might there be in the fact that this manipulative statement closes the book on Rebekah's life as far as Scripture is concerned?

> Only a gracious God could use an imperfect woman to accomplish his perfect will.
>
> Liz Curtis Higgs in *Slightly Bad Girls of the Bible*, page 147

8. What's the most important lesson you learned from our second visit with Rebekah, a mother who cared only about the end, not the means?

6

The Night Has Eyes

Leah the Unseen

Leah never saw it coming. Neither did Rachel. Yet envy and strife arrived at their doorstep one day—not as a young college grad, like our fictional Jeffrey, but as an age-old struggle between beautiful and plain, loved and unloved, visible and invisible. We begin this chapter, as we must, with Jacob's journey to Haran and the forgiveness he found en route, standing at the foot of a ladder of angels that rose into the night sky. Jacob wasn't looking for God, yet God was definitely watching and waiting for Jacob. God finds us where we are, beloved—and that's especially good news for us strays and runaways, for us Slightly Bad Girls who secretly borrowed our sister's favorite sweater. And her favorite perfume. And her favorite beau.

1a. After he deceived his father and robbed his brother, Jacob deserved a prison term, not a pardon. Yet instead of enumerating his crimes, God told Jacob, "I am with you" (**Genesis 28:15**). What a promise! When we studied Hagar and Ishmael, we learned "God was with the boy" (**Genesis 21:20**), just as God was "with" Joseph, Samson, Samuel, and Solomon. As they say on television, "But wait. There's more!" In the following passages whom did God promise to be with, and what did he say would accompany his presence in each case?

Genesis 26:24–25

Exodus 33:14–17

b. How can we know without a doubt that God will watch over us, as he did these ancient believers? What encouragement do you find in **Psalm 32:8** and **Matthew 28:19–20**?

c. Jacob had a vision of God at the top of that ladder and a very real sense of God's presence. **Genesis 28:16** records Jacob's response. Jot down those awe-filled words here.

I've never seen a ladder of angels, but I *have* had a sense of God's presence, often in the most unexpected places. Have you as well? Take a moment to describe your experience.

d. What evidence do we have of God's presence? As a possible answer, find a key word the following verses have in common: **Psalm 16:11, 1 Thessalonians 3:9,** and **Jude 24.** How does that word fit with your own experience of God's presence?

e. According to **Psalm 101:7,** a man like Jacob wouldn't be welcome
in David's presence, let alone God's. Yet the Lord willingly remained
with Jacob, knowing all the chicanery that preceded this encounter
in the night. How can a perfect, holy God have fellowship with
imperfect, unholy people?

f. Once you've considered your answer, study **Isaiah 41:8–10,** which
sums up God's relationship with Jacob in three powerful verses.
Note all the words God uses to describe this descendant of Abraham and his relationship with him.

Does the fact that God forgave Jacob so freely make you mad or
give you hope? Why is that?

g. Write out your own definition of the word *grace*. (It's not cheating
to have your Bible open to **Titus 3:4–7** while you jot down your
thoughts!)

God is *with* us. Not simply present by the power of the
Holy Spirit, he is *with* us, he is *for* us, he is *on our side.*
Liz Curtis Higgs in *Slightly Bad Girls of the Bible,* page 157

2a. God continued to be with Jacob on his journey north. At the well outside Haran, Jacob was outgoing and talkative with the shepherds, then impulsively moved the rock, kissed Rachel, and burst into tears. What reasons might you offer for his exuberant behavior?

b. Do you keep your emotions under wraps, as quiet Leah seemed to, or are you the effusive type, like Rachel, who ran home to Haran, bursting to share the news of her cousin's arrival?

c. How can God use each personality style for his glory? Read **Romans 12:6–8, Romans 11:29,** and **1 Corinthians 12:4–6,** then share your thoughts.

d. Laban was equally effusive in his greeting, described in **Genesis 29:13.** This isn't the first time we've met Rebekah's brother (see **Genesis 24:29–31**). How would you explain his warm welcome here?

e. Before we move on, skim through **Genesis 29:1–14** and notice who has disappeared from our story. Someone who we know was with Jacob and yet who seems to have been forgotten. What might that tell us about Laban's household?

> After a month of living with his nephew, Laban must have
> known what sort of payment Jacob would request.
>
> Liz Curtis Higgs in *Slightly Bad Girls of the Bible*, page 164

3a. "Tell me what your wages should be" (**Genesis 29:15**) is a strange
introduction to Leah and Rachel, our final two Slightly Bad Girls.
Yet that's what they would soon become to Jacob: payment in kind.
What does the wages-daughters connection tell us about their
father, Laban?

b. On page 165 of *Slightly Bad Girls of the Bible*, I explain the meaning of their names. Note the information here, then below each one
include a few characteristics of that animal that might hint at the
corresponding sister's appearance, temperament, or usefulness.

Leah means _____, which suggests:

Rachel means _____, which suggests:

c. Considering his daughters were named for livestock, Laban certainly deserved to have **Proverbs 12:10** written over the doorframe
of his home! In what ways does that verse fit his nature?

d. When we first met Esau and Jacob in **Genesis 25:27,** the brothers were defined by their labors: Esau was a long-range hunter; Jacob was a close-to-home shepherd. Yet in **Genesis 29:17** Leah and Rachel were defined by their appearance: one with gentle eyes, the other with beautiful everything. Are men today still defined by their work? And women by their looks? What makes you say that?

e. In describing yourself, is your *first* thought what you do ("I'm a mother," "I'm a teacher") or how you look ("I'm blond," "I'm petite")? Why might that be the case?

f. Comparing ourselves to others can stir up feelings of worthlessness and inadequacy *or* make us prideful and egotistical. In other words, proceed with caution! What do the following passages teach us about making comparisons?

2 Corinthians 10:12; 10:18

Galatians 2:6

Leah's eyes were apparently her only distinguishing feature. Her sister was another story.
Liz Curtis Higgs in *Slightly Bad Girls of the Bible,* page 166

4a. We've only just met Leah and Rachel, but you've probably already formed some opinion about them. At this point in the story, which sister garners your sympathy more, and why?

b. Putting a twenty-first-century spin on this sibling relationship, do you sense that Leah had self-esteem issues? Why or why not?

c. What advice do the following verses offer those of us who struggle with feelings of inadequacy and envy?

Galatians 5:26

1 Peter 4:8

d. We'll see their sibling rivalry in full tilt by chapter 8. Maybe the seeds were planted when Leah and Rachel were children; then watered when they caught a glimpse of themselves, side by side, in a polished bronze mirror; then nurtured when Laban pitted them against each other whenever it suited him. If you have a sibling (or two), what are your differences and similarities? In the simple grid on the next page, jot down your observations.

DIFFERENCES   **SIMILARITIES**

You

Sibling

Sibling

e. As you and your sibling(s) grew up, did people compare you to each other? What was that like for you?

In what ways did you compare yourself to your sibling(s)? What feelings did such comparisons arouse in you? Did you generally feel superior or inferior, and why?

f. Describe your relationship with your sibling(s) now. What has brought you closer over the last five years? And what, if anything, has driven you apart?

g. **Matthew 18:15** offers advice for mending fences. Can you picture that approach working in your family? Why or why not?

"Older" doesn't mean ancient. And "tender-eyed" doesn't mean unattractive.

Liz Curtis Higgs in *Slightly Bad Girls of the Bible,* page 165

5a. Like Sarah's much-discussed laugh, Leah's eyes have drawn significant attention from commentators. The Hebrew word *rakkoth*— translated as "weak" in the NIV, "pretty" in the NLT—has several meanings, including more positive connotations elsewhere in the Old Testament. Take a look at the following verses in which *rakkoth* describes someone or something.

In **Genesis 18:7** the calf is:

In **Genesis 33:13** the children are:

In **Deuteronomy 28:54** the man is:

In **Proverbs 15:1** the answer is:

How does this understanding affect your opinion of Leah's eyes?

b. Before you began this study, how did you picture Leah—her age, body type, features? On what was your opinion based?

c. Many of us imagined her as plain, even homely, but in truth Leah may have been quite lovely. Yet she paled next to her more beautiful sister. Whatever their appearance, "Jacob was in love with Rachel" (**Genesis 29:18**). What reasons would you suggest for Jacob favoring Rachel over Leah *other* than appearance?

d. The bargain was Jacob's own—"I'll work for you seven years in return for your younger daughter Rachel" (**Genesis 29:18**). Why would he offer twice the usual bride price, do you suppose?

e. Jacob was a man on a mission, with a clear directive from his father: "Take a wife for yourself there, from among the daughters of Laban" (**Genesis 28:2**). Yet elsewhere in Scripture, we find cautionary words about marriage. In **1 Corinthians 7:32–35** what concerns are identified for individuals in each of the following matrimonial states?

An unmarried man

A married man

An unmarried woman

A married woman

Was Paul suggesting we all remain single? What do you see as the point of this New Testament passage?

f. In the Old Testament, **1 Kings 11:4** addresses the same concern. If you're married, when have you felt your interests divided between pleasing your husband and pleasing the Lord? How did you resolve the issue?

g. Laban was all in favor of marriage, though his cryptic response— "It's better that I give her to you than to some other man" (**Genesis 29:19**)—should have alerted Jacob to the man's underhanded ways. What comparisons can you draw between Jacob and his father, who was ripe for deception because of his physical blindness and because he ignored what his functional senses were telling him?

Genesis 29:20 gives us a clue why Jacob didn't sense trouble on the horizon. No question, the man was smitten. In what ways does love sometimes blind us?

h. Now read **Genesis 29:21.** After seven years' labor, how could Jacob carelessly not ask for Rachel by name? **Proverbs 29:20** neatly states the problem. Think of a time when you spoke or acted in haste. What was the result, and what did you learn from the experience?

Isaac was blinded by age, but Jacob was blinded by love.

Liz Curtis Higgs in *Slightly Bad Girls of the Bible,* page 167

6a. On Jacob's wedding night, deception ran rampant. According to **Genesis 29:22,** who was running the show? Based on the bridal traditions described on page 170 of *Slightly Bad Girls of the Bible,* what elements were used to mask the switch, and why were they effective?

ELEMENT	EFFECTIVENESS

b. A less tangible yet even more powerful element belongs on the list: desire. Read **Romans 7:8,** then consider how Laban used Jacob's (and perhaps Leah's) desires to his advantage.

c. In **Genesis 29:23** the words *took* and *gave* serve as grim reminders
    of Laban's heartless manipulation. We've seen this taking and giving
    before. Read the passages below and note in each instance who did
    the taking, what each took, to whom it was given, and to what end.

Genesis 3:6

Genesis 16:3

What common elements, if any, do you notice in this sort of
taking and giving?

d. Have you ever taken something that was not yours and given it to
    someone else, thinking only of how you might benefit? Spend a
    moment rummaging through your memory bank. If something
    comes to mind (sad to say, it did for me), confess that sin to the
    Lord and seek his forgiveness.

e. What explanation can you offer for Rachel's absence in the wedding-
    night scene? Why might she have willingly stayed away?

f. Did Leah indeed show us her Slightly Bad Girl side that night? Or did Laban leave her no choice since fathers held sway over their families in these ancient societies? Explain your answer.

How does **Colossians 3:21** apply to a father like Laban?

What could Laban have told Leah to force her into Jacob's tent?

g. On page 172 of *Slightly Bad Girls of the Bible*, I suggest Leah might have harbored some affection for Jacob. Do you agree or disagree, and why?

Even if Leah was madly in love with Jacob, her actions cannot be sanctioned. How might **James 4:17** apply to Leah's situation that night?

h. What would you have done in her sandals? Should Leah have refused? Run away? Told Jacob? Found Rachel?

How can the encouragement we find in **James 4:7** and **1 Peter 5:8–10** help us when we find ourselves trapped in what seems like a no-win situation?

> All of Leah was concealed under that veil—her appearance, her emotions, her intentions, her desires, her hopes, her fears.
>
> Liz Curtis Higgs in *Slightly Bad Girls of the Bible*, page 171

7a. This deception scene hearkens back to the earlier tragedy in Isaac's tent. Compare the stories from **Genesis 27:5–29** and **Genesis 29:15–24,** using the grid below.

	DECEIVING ISAAC	DECEIVING JACOB
Scene of the crime		
Players involved		
Wardrobe changes		
Food and drink served		
Conferring of a blessing		

b. What similarities in style do you see between the true deceivers in these stories: Rebekah and Laban?

In what respects does **John 3:19** describe both Rebekah and Laban?

c. Rebekah deceived Isaac to procure a blessing for her son, while Laban deceived Jacob to nab a blessing for himself. Does that lessen the severity of Rebekah's crime? Or increase the severity of Laban's?

What difference, if any, does motive make in the eyes of God when it comes to sin? What does **Proverbs 21:2** suggest?

d. What do the tools of deception in these scenes—Jacob in Canaan, Leah in Haran—have in common, and how do they differ? Consider Jacob's and Leah's culpability, their willingness, their motives, their methods.

	JACOB	**LEAH**
Culpability		
Willingness		
Motive		
Methods		

e. Which are you more likely to be—the instigator, like Rebekah and Laban, or the compliant tool, like Jacob and Leah? Is one sin worse than the other? What assurance do we have in **Psalm 103:2–3**?

> Even if Laban was the one who *took* and *gave,* Leah was party to his deception.
>
> Liz Curtis Higgs in *Slightly Bad Girls of the Bible,* page 172

8. What's the most important lesson you learned from our initial visit with Leah, an unseen sister veiled in darkness?

7

Morning Has Broken

Leah the Unloved

I confess, I'm a morning person and love tiptoeing around a quiet house just before sunrise, easing my way into the day. That's why I hate alarm clocks. *Rrrinnnggg!* Very rude. Which brings us to a different kind of wake-up call altogether. Hours after the last partygoer stumbled home, the first rays of light bathed the goatskin walls of Jacob's tent. Did he reach for his sleeping bride, then recoil in horror? Or did Leah awaken first and pray for mercy? We can be certain only about what happened next.

1a. **Genesis 29:25** makes the surprise factor clear. Who had the ruder awakening: Jacob, discovering he'd married the wrong woman, or Leah, realizing her husband hated, despised, and rejected her? Make a case for each one, using the following verses for support, if you choose.

    Jacob had a heartbreaking morning because…
    Psalm 13:2; Micah 7:8

    Leah had a heartbreaking morning because…
    Psalm 69:19–20; Psalm 73:14

b. If they spoke at all that first morning, what do you imagine the newlywed couple said to each other?

Or do you think Jacob went directly to Laban's tent without speaking to Leah? What makes you say that?

c. As we see in **Genesis 29:25,** Jacob hammered Laban with three questions, not letting him get a word in edgewise. Did Jacob seem more upset about being deceived or about having Leah for a wife? On what do you base your answer?

d. What's ironic about Jacob's closing complaint to his uncle?

e. Often those of us with control issues also tend to be judgmental. What does **Matthew 7:1–5** teach us about seeing the sins in others and not in ourselves?

If judging others is one of your weaknesses (it's definitely one of mine), how can you "take the plank out of your own eye" so you can see your sins more clearly? Think of some practical solutions, such as keeping a journal or having an accountability partner.

f. Think of a time when you were betrayed or deceived in some way. Was it the motive or the method or the outcome that bothered you most? Why?

g. Jacob turned to Laban for an explanation rather than turning to God. To whom do you imagine Leah turned for counsel? How might **Psalm 88:13** fit this situation?

> When we're wronged, we don't care *how* someone managed to trick us; we want to know *why* we've been beguiled.
>
> Liz Curtis Higgs in *Slightly Bad Girls of the Bible*, page 182

2a. Check out Laban's flimsy excuse for substituting Leah for Rachel in **Genesis 29:26.** He doesn't even bother to name his daughters. To him they're just _____ and _____. Things don't improve in **verse 27,** where he refers to them as _____ and _____. Does such shoddy treatment indicate a cultural bias against women, or does it merely reveal Laban's callous attitude toward his daughters? Or both?

b. The girls' mother is never mentioned in Scripture, though Jewish tradition gives her the name Adinah. If Laban's wife was still living, she certainly stayed in the background. How might a stronger mother have altered the father-daughter relationships in this family?

c. Even if Leah knew a mother's love, she did not know Jacob's love, as **Genesis 29:30** makes clear. How does your translation word the phrase contrasting Jacob's feelings for Rachel with his feelings for Leah?

Do you see any hope for Leah in those words? Why or why not?

d. Should Jacob have tried harder to love both wives? Put aside Leah? Put aside Rachel? Hightailed it back to Canaan? What options did Jacob have other than to accept Laban's solution?

e. Leah was given no options at all. Based on your own experience or observation, describe what happens over time in a one-sided relationship.

f. For half a century *Ladies' Home Journal* has featured the column "Can This Marriage Be Saved?" If Leah submitted a letter asking that question, what would she write about Jacob?

What advice might a modern marital therapist give this unloved wife?

g. By contrast, what advice would God's timeless, flawless Word offer her? Find a biblical word of encouragement for Leah on your own, then see what these verses have to offer.

Psalm 119:141

Proverbs 3:3–4

1 Peter 3:1–2

Beloved, just because the Lord is silent doesn't mean he's distant. God misses nothing.

Liz Curtis Higgs in *Slightly Bad Girls of the Bible*, page 186

3a. In *Matthew Henry's Commentary on the Whole Bible*, Rev. Henry noted, "Jacob was paid in his own coin," though I believe Leah bore the greater cost. Do you agree, or did all three spouses suffer equally?

b. Make a case for Jacob bearing the greatest burden, trying to please two women.

c. Now carry the banner for Rachel as the injured party, sharing the husband she thought would be hers alone.

d. Finally, defend Leah as the worst treated of the three, married to a man who did not love her.

e. Here are three verses, carefully chosen to suit Jacob, Leah, and Rachel. Whom would you match with each verse, and why?

FITS WITH...   BECAUSE...

James 3:14

Psalm 119:50

Psalm 38:4

f. When we're in a difficult situation, it's easy to see how we've been wronged—and harder to spot how we might have wronged someone else. Choose a challenging relationship in your own life and consider what the other person has endured.

g. What counsel does God's Word provide for enduring such challenges?

Romans 5:3–4

Ephesians 4:32

We don't know what that week held for these two ill-matched partners, but we can be certain sorrow and shame played a large part.

Liz Curtis Higgs in *Slightly Bad Girls of the Bible*, page 184

4a. The pivotal verse in our story is this one: "When the LORD saw that Leah was not loved..." (**Genesis 29:31**). How did that phrase strike you the first time you read it?

b. Does the realization that God sees inside your heart and knows the intimate details of your life encourage you or make you uncomfortable? Why might that be so?

c. The following verses give us pause, reminding us how closely God
examines our hearts. Note what each reveals about how and why
the Lord does so.

Psalm 139:23–24

Hebrews 4:12

Jeremiah 17:10

d. We're also assured that, even knowing us intimately, God loves us.
How do the following verses calm your fears about his knowing
every inch of your heart?

Deuteronomy 30:6

Psalm 73:26

Acts 15:8

e. Leah is never called barren, yet according to **Genesis 29:31,** God
did open, or bless, her womb, altering her status from unloved to
beloved. In her time and place, the ability to bear children was a
sure sign of God's regard. Here and now, how could God best
express love to you?

f. Leah's first recorded words coincide with the birth of her first son in
    Genesis 29:32. Notice she began with the Lord's name, giving him
    credit. Do you think Leah had a strong relationship with God all
    along, or when he opened her womb, do you think he also opened
    the door of her heart? Explain how you came to that conclusion.

g. God changed Leah's life forever when he answered her prayers.
    What changes do you long for in your life that only God could
    orchestrate?

> The Lord's gaze fell on a quiet, unassuming woman who
> needed what only he could provide.
>
> Liz Curtis Higgs in *Slightly Bad Girls of the Bible*, page 187

5a. **Genesis 29:32** ends with Leah's poignant plea for affection. Even
    loved by God as she was, Leah longed for Jacob's love too. Was
    that a realistic expectation on her part or simply an indication of
    spiritual or emotional immaturity? What makes you say that?

b. Skim through **Genesis 29:33–35.** Do you find any response from
    Jacob? For that matter is anyone mentioned other than Leah and
    her sons? What does that suggest about Leah's day-to-day life?

c. What themes do you imagine echoed through Leah's prayers? See if **Psalm 25:16** provides any ideas.

d. Though she pined for her husband's love, there's no mention of Leah's desiring her sister's affection or her forgiveness. How would you explain that?

We also have no record of Leah taunting Rachel during her pregnancies, as Hagar did Sarai, nor flaunting her newborn children in front of her barren sister. What does that tell us about Leah?

e. If you were the older, unloved sister with a beautiful, much-loved sibling, how would you resist the urge to show off God's abundant blessings? (I'm telling you right now, *this* Former Bad Girl would be sorely tempted to dress my baby boys in matching outfits and parade them across my sister's lawn on a pony!)

f. Leah, by example, shows us how to live out the following verses: **Matthew 11:29, Philippians 2:3,** and **Ephesians 4:2.** Any one of the three would make a terrific memory verse. Choose one and copy it here, then commit the words to heart.

> Leah knew she was not alone, knew her life was not with-
> out purpose.
>
> Liz Curtis Higgs in *Slightly Bad Girls of the Bible*, page 193

6a. Leah's emergence from the shadows of her Slightly Bad Girl maid-
    enhood to her Mostly Good Girl motherhood is encouraging to
    watch. Though another millennium would pass before David's
    psalms were circulated and sung, I can almost hear the words of
    Psalm 56:4 and **Psalm 118:17** pouring from Leah's heart as she
    went about her work. How is joy possible in the midst of difficult
    circumstances?

 b. Though no response from Jacob is recorded in Scripture, he obvi-
    ously spent at least *some* time with Leah because another son soon
    filled her arms. **Genesis 29:33** finds her once again acknowledging
    God: "Because the LORD heard that I am not loved…" What might
    the distinction between "the LORD saw" and "the LORD heard" sug-
    gest about Leah's spiritual life?

 c. How do **Psalm 34:15** and **Deuteronomy 26:7** assure you that the
    Lord both sees *and* hears you?

 d. We know at least a year unfolded between the advent of Leah's
    sons, yet in Scripture the births come one after another. **Genesis**

29:34 doesn't bother to hide the repetition: "Again she conceived…" However, this time Leah's response was a bit different: "Now at last my husband will become attached to me." Why do you suppose Leah looked to Jacob after Levi's birth rather than to the Lord?

e. Do we have any indication that Jacob became attached to her other than physically?

f. A physical relationship alone does not make a marriage. What do you most long for in a relationship with a man?

g. If you've been disappointed in some way, as Leah was, **Romans 15:13** outlines a clear path to hope, joy, and peace. What does this verse ask you to do? And where will you find the power to do that?

> Her God was with her. Her sons were with her. And before another season passed, her womb was full again.
>
> Liz Curtis Higgs in *Slightly Bad Girls of the Bible*, page 193

7a. **Genesis 29:35** begins with the familiar refrain "She conceived again." But this time was different. This time Leah didn't look to

Jacob for love; she'd already found it. Speak aloud Leah's bold decla-
ration in that verse, then jot down how it must have felt for her to
finally say those words…and how it feels for you to say them.

b. We often find this verb *praise* in psalms of thanksgiving, and we
    certainly hear gratitude in Leah's voice. How do the following verses
    expand your understanding of what it means to praise the Lord?

    Isaiah 37:16

    Psalm 96:4

    Revelation 15:4

c. "She named him Judah" (**Genesis 29:35**), a name that resounds
    throughout God's Word, from first book to last. At the end of his life,
    Jacob spoke a prophetic blessing over Judah. Read **Genesis 49:10.**
    Two key biblical characters would fulfill this prophecy. See if you can
    name them on your own, then turn to the verses to confirm.

    (1)
    2 Samuel 7:8; 2 Samuel 7:16; 2 Chronicles 6:6

    (2)
    Matthew 2:6; Revelation 5:5

d. Leah could not know of the glory to come in her lineage, just as we cannot know what blessings and honor may come to our offspring. Why is it best that God alone knows such things?

e. According to **Psalm 100:5** and **Psalm 135:13,** what will endure forever, through all generations?

f. A profile in *The Woman's Study Bible* observes, "Leah personified for every woman the crucial need to live primarily for God and His glory." Why might doing so make a difference in our lives?

Practically speaking, how can you put God first as Leah finally did?

With a heart full of joy, Leah lifted her voice to the One who mattered most.

Liz Curtis Higgs in *Slightly Bad Girls of the Bible*, page 193

8. What's the most important lesson you learned from our second visit with Leah, an unloved wife who was very much loved by God?

8

When All Is Said and Done

Rachel

After spending two chapters with our *un*seen, *un*loved Leah, we may find ourselves feeling *un*sympathetic toward Rachel. She's beautiful to behold and deeply loved. How dare she be jealous of poor Leah! But she was, and (if we're honest) we understand why. First, two women cannot share one man; the human heart isn't wired for it. And second, Leah had what Rachel wanted most: children. In *Matthew Henry's Commentary on the Whole Bible*, Rev. Henry wrote, "See what roots of bitterness envy and strife are, and what mischief they make among relations." That's the perfect description of our final Slightly Bad Girl: *mischievous.*

1a. With a handful of words, the ugly picture comes into focus: "Rachel…became jealous of her sister" (**Genesis 30:1**). The color green is associated with fertility, with life. But in Rachel's case, green was most unbecoming. How does envy affect people—mind, body, and soul—according to **Proverbs 14:30** and your own experience?

James 3:16 warns us about other things envy produces. In what ways is that fruit evident in Rachel's life?

b. When Rachel blasted Jacob in **Genesis 30:1,** the bitterness in her voice was unmistakable. We find similar feelings expressed in **Job 7:11.** Why do bitterness and emotional venting seem to go hand in hand?

c. Why do you think Rachel turned to her husband with her heartache rather than to God? What might that tell us about Rachel's relationship with the Lord?

d. It's not enough to consider Rachel's jealous nature; we must also examine our own. Whom do you find yourself envying? Family members? Friends? Co-workers? Strangers?

What specific situations push your buttons, and why?

What do you long for that you don't have?

e. We noticed that Rachel's envy sprang from the root of idolatry. Dig a little deeper, dear sister. What might lie beneath your envy?

What does **1 Corinthians 13:4** suggest is the antidote for envy?

f. Are you ready to ask God to pull out that root—far more stubborn than a mandrake—and plant contentment in your life? To prepare the soil of your heart, consider the following passages and, based on the truth each verse offers, note what contentment might look and feel like for you.

Proverbs 19:23

1 Timothy 6:6

Hebrews 13:5

> Whenever we compare our life to another woman's, we're bound to see something we want but can't have.
>
> Liz Curtis Higgs in *Slightly Bad Girls of the Bible*, page 205

2a. As we see in **Genesis 30:2,** Jacob's response to Rachel's demand was immediate—and vitriolic. Anger is a common emotion in the Bible, being mentioned hundreds of times. In many cases, such as **Deuteronomy 6:14–15,** God is the One burning with divine, righteous anger. What does **Psalm 37:8** tell us to do with our human, unrighteous anger?

b. With whom do you think Jacob was angry, and why? The Lord? Rachel? Leah? Himself? Make a case for the one you believe Jacob most blamed for his misery.

c. When Jacob asked his whiny wife, "Am I in the place of God" (**Genesis 30:2**), he spoke in anger, but he also spoke the truth. He could not do what God could do; he could not take God's place. What unspoken thoughts might have been behind Jacob's rebuke?

d. Rachel should have turned to the Lord, but she turned to her husband instead. If you've ever put all your trust in someone, expecting that person, in essence, to be God for you, how did he or she respond?

And what did you learn from the experience?

e. What do **Psalm 146:3, Psalm 20:7,** and **Isaiah 26:4** teach us about where we should and should not put our trust?

f. When Jacob couldn't solve her problem, Rachel did a rash and foolish thing. Playing the role of God, she ordered her husband to sleep with her maidservant so she could create life, as it were, so she could have children. If Rachel were standing before you, what cautionary word would you give her about such a plan?

g. Compare Rachel's motives and methods to Sarai's two generations earlier.

What Sarai Said	What Abram Did
Genesis 16:2	

What Rachel Said	What Jacob Did
Genesis 30:3–4	

What do these similar passages demonstrate about human nature?

Rachel's intentions weren't as honorable as her great-aunt's: Sarai wanted an heir for Abram; Rachel wanted children for Rachel, period.

Liz Curtis Higgs in *Slightly Bad Girls of the Bible*, pages 207–8

3a. Rachel's response to the birth of her sons through her servant was very different from Sarai's seeming indifference, even anger, toward Ishmael. Look at **Genesis 30:6** and **Genesis 30:8,** then jot down the words of triumph and victory pouring from Rachel's mouth.

b. On page 209 of *Slightly Bad Girls of the Bible,* I suggest (as do other commentators) that Rachel sounded boastful. Do you agree or disagree, and why?

Why was Rachel's experience with a surrogate mother so different from Sarai's, do you think?

c. **Genesis 30:9** finds Leah jumping into the fray even though she already had four sons of her own. What was this about, do you imagine? Jealousy on Leah's part? A spirit of competitiveness? Or was she merely following social dictates by providing more sons for her husband?

d. Leah chose names for her sons that revealed her elation at their births. Note each name in **Genesis 30:11** and **Genesis 30:13.** How did you feel when Leah joined her sister in the Great Baby Battle?

e. Rachel and Leah's first conversation in Scripture, recorded in **Genesis 30:14–15,** brings us to a high point in the story, full of tension and drama. But spiritually, the sisters had reached a low point. Read aloud their dialogue, provided below—with a partner if you're in a small group—then note what hidden thoughts, emotions, and desires might have prompted each of their comments.

Rachel: "Please give me some of your son's mandrakes."

Leah: "Wasn't it enough that you took away my husband? Will you take my son's mandrakes too?"

Rachel: "Very well, he can sleep with you tonight in return for your son's mandrakes."

f. When you first read the mandrake scene, were you rooting for Leah (pun intended), glad she'd finally spoken her mind to Rachel and then to Jacob (**Genesis 30:16**)? Or were you dismayed to see the lengths to which these women went for children? What do you imagine Jacob's reaction was to all this?

g. In our day we may not amass offspring to impress our neighbors, but most of us surely collect something. What's your keeping-up-with-the-Joneses temptation, that *thing* you just can't get enough of?

To what lengths have you gone to add another one of those gotta-have-it items to your life?

Read the verses on the following page, noting what God might be calling you to change about your behavior in light of the truth revealed in his Word.

Luke 12:15

Matthew 6:19–21

1 John 3:17

h. We learn in **Genesis 30:17–21** that "God listened to Leah" and blessed her womb again. What do those verses reveal about Leah's relationship with Jacob? And, more to the point, her relationship with God?

> As for Rachel, the mandrakes not only didn't work, they backfired: two more sons for Leah and a daughter as well.
>
> Liz Curtis Higgs in *Slightly Bad Girls of the Bible*, pages 216–17

4a. Finally "God remembered Rachel" (**Genesis 30:22**). Such a tender phrase. What does that mean to you, to be remembered by God?

b. On page 217 of *Slightly Bad Girls of the Bible,* we learned that both David and the criminal on the cross beseeched God, "Remember me"—a common plea throughout Scripture. Consider two more examples in the Old Testament, noting the specific request connected with each "remember me."

REQUEST OF GOD

Hannah: **1 Samuel 1:10–11**

Nehemiah: **Nehemiah 13:14**

Which of these requests do you identify with, and why?

c. Sometimes when we ask God to remember us, we're also asking him to forget something: our sins. Look at **Psalm 25:7.** Is there something you would ask God *not* to remember about your life?

Rest assured, the Lord already knows and stands ready to forgive. And forget. In case you're thinking, *God can't forget anything!* check out **Hebrews 8:12** for an encouraging word on that score. What does it say, and what does that mean for you?

d. When God remembered Rachel, "he listened to her and opened her womb" (**Genesis 30:22**). As with Leah, if God was listening, then Rachel must have been praying—if not begging and pleading, knowing our dramatic Rachel! How might God's delay in opening her womb have benefited Rachel spiritually?

e. In what ways does **Joel 2:12–13** seem to be a hand-in-glove fit for our humbled Rachel, finally turning toward God instead of trying to *be* God? Note five things we are called to *do* in this passage and five things God promises to *be*.

WE ARE CALLED TO...

(1)

(2)

(3)

(4)

(5)

Which of those actions would be the most challenging for you, and why?

AND GOD WILL BE...

(1)

(2)

(3)

(4)

(5)

Which of these attributes of God gives you sufficient courage to "return to the LORD your God" (**Joel 2:13**)?

f. Rachel prayed, God answered, and a son was born, removing her disgrace (**Genesis 30:23**). For Rachel, the Lord took away not only the societal disgrace of barrenness but also the shame of her sin. What assurances do **Isaiah 50:7, Isaiah 25:8,** and **Revelation 21:4** offer about God's ability to do the same for us?

Beloved, what tears, what sorrows, what shame in your life are you praying that God will take away today?

> From the moment God opened her womb, Rachel knew she was remembered, accepted, and blessed.
>
> Liz Curtis Higgs in *Slightly Bad Girls of the Bible*, page 218

5a. With eleven(!) sons to raise, Jacob's household stayed busy while the patriarch put his shepherding skills to good use. "The man grew exceedingly prosperous" (**Genesis 30:43**), which did not thrill his father-in-law, Laban. Time to go, bro. Reading **Genesis 31:3,** note the Lord's timely response.

God's *command* to Jacob:

God's *promise* to Jacob:

b. Surely Jacob had not intended to remain in Haran for twenty long years. Why do you suppose he didn't act sooner?

In **Hosea 12:3,** what did the prophet say of Jacob? Did it seem that struggle was finally over? Explain your answer.

c. In Genesis 31 Rachel and Leah listened to a rather lengthy discourse from Jacob about how Laban had deceived him. (No kidding!) Finally the sisters spoke, revealing how they felt about their father. According to **Genesis 31:14–16,** what did they object to most, and why?

Were the sisters being greedy or demanding what was rightfully theirs?

d. What does **Proverbs 13:22** tell us about who inherits a Bad Boy's money?

How might the wisdom of **Proverbs 28:25** apply to Jacob and the facts presented in **Genesis 30:43–31:1**?

e. If you've been through any inheritance situations in your family, what did you learn about your parents? Your siblings? Yourself?

f. Laban's accusations in **Genesis 31:26–28** are almost laughable. What did Laban accuse Jacob of doing? And why is Laban's dismay rather unbelievable?

g. With **1 Peter 3:9** in mind, explain how Jacob could have dislodged his family from Haran in a more honorable way than we find in **Genesis 31:20.**

> When we choose our timing to avoid getting caught, something isn't quite…um, kosher.
>
> Liz Curtis Higgs in *Slightly Bad Girls of the Bible*, page 222

6a. In the middle of Jacob's getaway scene appears a brief but significant fact, recorded in **Genesis 31:19.** Why would Rachel have done such a risky thing?

We know "Laban had gone to shear his sheep" (**Genesis 31:19**), so the coast was clear. Still, was her thievery a premeditated act, or did Rachel grab the teraphim on impulse? Defend your stance.

b. The problem wasn't simply that they were stolen; these household idols defiled anyone who touched them. Read **Deuteronomy 29:17–18** and summarize the admonishment you find there.

c. If you've ever taken something from another person as an act of spite or revenge, what did you learn about yourself—and human nature—in the process?

d. What do **Leviticus 19:18** and **Romans 12:19** teach us to do when the urge to take revenge strikes?

e. When Laban demanded, "But why did you steal my gods?" (**Genesis 31:30**), things really got hairy (**Genesis 31:32**). Do you believe Jacob would have killed Rachel rather than break a solemn vow?

What do **Numbers 30:2** and **Ecclesiastes 5:5** tell us about the seriousness of vows?

f. Read **Genesis 31:32–37,** a scene brimming with dramatic tension. However amusing (and effective) Rachel's clever time-of-the-month ploy, she'd unwittingly beckoned death to her door twice, first with "Give me children, or I'll die!" (**Genesis 30:1**), then with Jacob's vow in **Genesis 31:32.** Some might say she was tempting God, yet what does **James 1:13** remind us?

Do you think Rachel's Slightly Bad Girl behavior in any way contributed to her tragic demise? What makes you say that?

> Right and wrong are timeless, and what Rachel did was Bad-Girl wrong.
>
> Liz Curtis Higgs in *Slightly Bad Girls of the Bible,* page 222

7a. Though we were with Rachel when "she breathed her last" (**Genesis 35:18**), she remains in our hearts as the lovely young shepherdess who greeted her cousin by the well and set in motion one of the most vivid stories in Scripture. How have your feelings about Rachel changed from her first scene to her last?

b. Certainly Rachel is one of the more memorable characters in the Bible, with *character* being the operative word. Her flaws were many, but so were her strengths. Take a moment to list them.

HER FLAWS   HER STRENGTHS

In your estimation how does she compare to our other Slightly Bad Girls? Who was the "baddest" of the five, and why?

c. If you had the power to undo something Rachel did or to change something about her nature, what would that be, and why?

d. Now look at your own life through a friend's eyes and answer the same questions. Which of your actions—those big bloopers, those major mistakes—would you undo, and why?

e. Though we cannot change our past, we can certainly shape our future. What character trait will you step back and let God refashion for your benefit?

f. We're told in **2 Corinthians 3:18** and **1 John 3:2** how we are transformed into God's likeness, both now and in that glorious day to come when "we shall see him as he is." In the meantime **Ephesians 4:22–24** advises us how to "put on the new self." Describe the "new self" you long to become, shaped by God's loving hands.

> God remembered her. And loved her. And blessed her—not because of any Good Girl deeds, but because of his great mercy.
>
> Liz Curtis Higgs in *Slightly Bad Girls of the Bible*, page 228

8. What's the most important lesson you learned from Rachel, the memorable mother of Joseph and Benjamin?

A Last Word from Liz

It's hard to say good-bye—both to you and to these five feisty women. How I've loved being part of the Ancient Sisterhood of the Traveling Tents!

Now when I meet a woman named Sarah or autograph a book to a Rebekah or see a wedding announcement for a Rachel, I will think of these Slightly Bad Girls and smile. And when I cross paths with a woman who's suffered at the hands of another or a wife who feels unloved or a mother who feels unappreciated, I will share the journeys of Hagar and Leah, two women whom God noticed when others did not.

I hope you feel the same way, sis, and that our time together through the pages of this *Slightly Bad Girls of the Bible* book and workbook have been valuable to you. May the stories of these five women reside in your heart, continuing to shape your life as the days unfold.

Please know that my readers are my best teachers, and I'm always honored to hear what you've discovered in our time together. Kindly write to me at:

Liz Curtis Higgs
P.O. Box 43577
Louisville, KY 40253-0577

Or visit my Web site:
www.LizCurtisHiggs.com

Until we meet across the page or in person, know that you are blessed by God and a blessing to others—including me!

* catholic priest for the poor
  name is